RAND EDUCATION

T0167770

Competency-Based Education Programs in Texas

An Innovative Approach to Higher Education

Lindsay Daugherty, Van Davis, Trey Miller

Sponsored by the College for All Texans Foundation

For more information on this publication, visit www.rand.org/t/RR1239

Library of Congress Cataloging-in-Publication Data
is available for this publication.

ISBN: 978-0-8330-9176-5

Published by the RAND Corporation, Santa Monica, Calif.
© Copyright 2015 RAND Corporation
RAND® is a registered trademark.

Cover Image: Fotolia©ktsdesign

Support RAND
Make a tax-deductible charitable contribution at
www.rand.org/giving/contribute

www.rand.org

Preface

Higher-education institutions in Texas are increasingly exploring innovative approaches to structuring and delivering degree programs. Several institutions have developed competency-based degree programs, which aim to offer new pathways for students to obtain postsecondary credentials and to reduce higher-education costs for students by focusing on mastery of competencies rather than on seat time. These programs often differ from traditional degree programs in a variety of ways; typically they include self-paced movement through courses, online course delivery, the exclusive reliance on assessments to demonstrate mastery of competencies, reorientation of faculty roles, enhanced student supports, and movement away from tuition structures that are tied to credit hours.

This report aims to describe existing competency-based degrees and certificate programs in Texas; to summarize the national landscape for competency-based programs, including the perceived benefits and limitations; and to suggest some potential areas for focus as the state of Texas and higher-education institutions explore the possibility of further expanding these programs. While this report was specifically written for Texas state policymakers and administrators at institutions in Texas, it may be informative to policymakers and higher-education leaders across the nation.

This report was funded by the Lumina Foundation through a grant to the College for All Texans Foundation. The research was conducted by RAND Education, with support from the Texas Higher Education Coordinating Board. Questions and comments can be sent to the project leader, Trey Miller, at tmiller@rand.org or by phone at (310) 503-5364.

Contents

CHAPTER FOUR

A Path Forward for Competency-Based Education in Texas 47

Box and Table

Box

Table

Summary

In recent years, the White House and other key stakeholders have raised concerns about the state of higher education and are calling for new, innovative approaches to address these concerns (Hart Research Associates, 2010; Lumina Foundation, 2013; White House, 2013). Concerns about higher education focus on the low rates of postsecondary success among students, a perceived lack of alignment between the skills of graduates and the needs of employers, and rapidly increasing costs for students.

Competency-based degree and certificate programs offer one response to concerns about costs, student success, relevancy, and value. These programs are reoriented to focus on the mastery of competencies to drive a student's progress through education as opposed to sequential completion of term-long courses. The purpose of this report is to inform state policymakers and institutional leaders in Texas about the landscape for competency-based education, including state-specific efforts and the larger national picture. We first conducted a literature review to describe what is currently known about competency-based programs. We then conducted interviews with program leadership at each of the six institutions with such offerings in Texas and with a sample of competency-based education students at one of these institutions. Given limited evidence, we are not able to assess the overall effectiveness of Texas programs, but we do discuss some lessons learned by the six target institutions. We also suggest some potential areas of focus for future research and policymaking that should be explored to provide evidence on the quality and cost of competency-based education and support the development of high-quality programs. The lessons learned around implementation and suggested areas of research and policy focus also may be useful to stakeholders outside of the state of Texas.

Key Features of Competency-Based Education

The literature and key stakeholder organizations in higher education define competency-based education in a variety of ways; however, most agree on at least one central feature: competency-based education focuses on what a student is expected to know and be able to do at the end of the course or program (i.e., "competencies") and awards course credit or a degree/certificate when the student has demonstrated mastery of these competencies (Bell and Conklin, 2013; Person, Goble, and Bruch, 2014; Porter and Reilly, 2014). Many traditional courses are designed with learning outcomes or competencies in mind, yet students are typically exposed to a common set of materials (e.g., syllabus, textbook, lecture topics) and are required to sit through full courses regardless of when the material is mastered. In contrast to traditional courses, competency-based programs allow for substantial variation in the content and structure used to achieve mastery of competencies. This understanding of competency-based education is echoed in the K–12 space, where the literature defines it according to five characteristics: (1) students advance upon mastery; (2) the competencies include explicit, measureable learning objectives; (3) assessment is meaningful and positive for students; (4) students receive timely, differentiated support based on individual needs; and (5) learning outcomes include application and creation of knowledge, along with the development of important skills and dispositions (Sturgis, 2015).

In higher education, competency-based programs vary from institution to institution, though programs typically involve some or all of the features described below.

- *Flexible scheduling and completion:* Students are typically able to complete coursework and assessments at variable paces. To facilitate self-paced movement through coursework, competency-based programs often offer more flexible calendars that allow students to end and begin new courses throughout a traditional course semester.

- *Online delivery of instruction*: Competency-based programs often rely on online platforms for course delivery and communication between faculty and students; online platforms allow for self-pacing and flexible scheduling through continuous access to learning materials.

- *Variation in course content:* Within and across programs, the material used by a student to master a competency may vary. Some students may not need to study material that they have previously mastered, and students may have choices of a range of different learning materials from which to choose (e.g., texts, videos, computer modules).

- *Exclusive emphasis on assessments linked to competencies*: Competency-based programs typically rely exclusively on a set of assessments as the sole means of determining mastery and moving students through the program, and these assessments are directly linked to the competencies mapped out for the full degree or certificate program. Institutions often use a range of assessment types within a single program or course, including computerized exams, projects, essays, research papers, problem solving, and demonstrations (Klein-Collins and Baylor, 2013). Students can take the assessments as soon as they feel they have mastered a competency.

- *Altered faculty roles:* Given the personalized, self-paced nature of competency-based learning, the roles of faculty differ from those played in traditional degree programs. Rather than lecturing, faculty members devote efforts to compiling and creating course materials, guiding students to materials that might be most useful in mastering competencies, providing students with instructional support and general guidance as they move through the program, and administering assessments and certifying results.

- *Strong student supports:* Given the significant autonomy students have, institutions often provide them with regular, comprehensive support through staff referred to as "coaches," who monitor and facilitate student progress and success.

- *Alternative tuition structures:* Some competency-based programs have adopted a subscription-based model of tuition, under which students pay a fixed price for a term and are able to complete as many courses as possible for that fixed price. This provides incentives for students to complete coursework as quickly as possible.

Benefits and Limitations of Competency-Based Education

Supporters of competency-based education argue that it addresses some of the concerns about the ability of higher education programs to meet employer needs and to increase rates of degree and certificate completion. Most competency-based programs aim to increase the alignment between graduate skills and employer needs through a focus on demonstrated competencies that are informed partially by employer needs. The programs are expected to provide greater assurance to employers that graduates hold the knowledge, skills, and abilities necessary for employment in particular areas. Competency-based education has the potential to address degree-completion rates by offering new pathways to students who might otherwise not have entered or completed a degree program. For example, the flexible, self-paced nature of the format is attractive to students with competing obligations, such as work and family responsibilities. Students with prior education and work experience can use their knowledge and experience to move through familiar competencies quickly, with the intent that they focus on new knowledge, skills, and abilities rather than competencies they have gained elsewhere. For students who move through the material at a quicker pace, particularly those in programs with subscription-based tuition, competency-based programs also offer the potential to obtain degrees and certificates at significantly lower costs to the student.

There are, however, also concerns about competency-based higher-education programs. Critics argue that these programs threaten traditional programs by diminishing enrollments, and that eliminating the central role of faculty in lecturing may lead to loss of faculty jobs (HCM Strategists, 2013, and Shapiro, 2014). In addition, some argue that these programs will not be provided at high levels of quality and will simply become "degree mills." There are particular concerns about the applied nature of the content and the modularized structure, and the impact this has on the ability to connect knowledge to theory, to translate competencies across settings, and to make connections across competencies (Mitchell and Bell, 2000, and O'Donoghue and Chapman, 2010). There are also concerns about the inability of these programs to provide some of the benefits that traditional programs offer beyond knowledge and skills (e.g., social interaction) (O'Donoghue and Chapman, 2010). Finally, given the high level of autonomy offered to students within the competency-based model, some have argued that it may be appropriate for adult learners and students with high levels of motivation and self-efficacy, but may be less appropriate for traditionally aged college students or those with developmental education needs (Person, Goble, and Bruch, 2014). These concerns regarding competency-based programs suggest that they may be useful to explore as an alternative pathway for certain fields and types of students, but should not necessarily supplant traditional programs.

Competency-Based Degree and Certificate Programs in Texas

There are six higher-education institutions in Texas that offer competency-based programs: Western Governors University (WGU), Texas A&M Commerce (TAMUC), South Texas College (STC), Texas State Technical College (TSTC), Austin Community College (ACC), and Lone Star College. Three of the programs offer bachelor's degrees, and three of the programs offer associate's degrees or certificates. One program also offers graduate degrees. The programs are largely focused in business or vocational areas, and many share common features.

To demonstrate mastery of a competency, each of the programs reported using a variety of types of assessments (e.g., portfolios, demonstrations, essays, traditional tests) and allowing students to take assessments whenever they think they are ready. Based on completion of these assessments, all of the programs offer the ability for students to complete courses at variable paces. The TSTC program is unique in that it is a direct-assessment program.[1] All other programs in Texas use course-based approaches that link competencies back to courses associated with credit hours.[2]

In addition, the roles of faculty and support staff are similar across most of the programs. Courses are no longer driven by lectures from instructors, and pathways through coursework are tailored to the needs of individual students. Instructors spend time developing and identifying course materials, providing individualized guidance to students as they work through different materials, and administering and grading assessments. In each of the six institutions, dedicated staff (i.e., coaches) assess progress and provide students with academic and nonacademic support as needed (e.g., helping to balance courses with employment responsibilities, providing motivation, troubleshooting administrative issues).

There are also a number of areas where programs differ. Four programs offer subscription-based tuition, while two continue to charge tuition by the credit hour. Half of the programs are entirely online, while the other half require some in-person interaction or instruction. Five of the programs have student populations that are made up primarily of older students with work or family obligations, but one of the programs enrolls a somewhat larger percentage of younger enrollees who enter straight from high school. In addition, four of the institutions have adopted a fully flexible calendar for competency-based offer-

---

[1]   According to the Southern Association of Colleges and Schools Commission on Colleges (SACSCOC), the regional accreditor for Texas colleges, "Federal regulations define a direct assessment competency-based educational program as an instructional program that, in lieu of credit hours or clock hours as a measure of student learning, uses direct assessment of student learning relying solely on the attainment of defined competencies, or recognizes the direct assessment of student learning by others." While course-based programs map competencies onto courses with credit-hour equivalents and develop programs that add up to traditional credit requirements for degree programs (e.g., 120 credits for a bachelor's degree), direct assessment programs do not do this mapping.

[2]   WGU technically uses competency units, but the website refers to these as "credit equivalents," and they are largely indistinguishable from credit hours.

ings that allows students to begin and end courses at any time, while two have retained terms that range from seven weeks to 16 weeks to align competency-based offerings with the calendars that have been created for traditional degree programs.

In addition to gathering general information on the programs, we had the opportunity to interview a group of students from one of the institutions. Although our interviews reflect experiences with only one institution, those interviewed generally had positive experiences. The most commonly cited benefits of the program included low cost, the convenience and flexibility of studying at one's own pace through an online platform, the ability to move more quickly through courses, and the more-applied focus that makes the material immediately usable in daily employment. Students also liked the subscription-based structure of tuition for the program. The few challenges students mentioned were problems with mathematics coursework, some inconsistency in experiences with instructors, and occasional challenges with technology or administrative processes. On the whole, however, students strongly preferred the competency-based program to traditional programs, and most had recommended these programs to others.

Challenges and Lessons Learned

According to interviews with administrators and students, institutions faced a number of challenges as they developed competency-based degree and certificate programs. These challenges fell in seven areas:

1. Integrating the programs into existing administrative tools and processes
2. Responding to oversight by the federal government and accreditors
3. Ensuring faculty buy-in and training
4. Developing the content for the programs
5. Providing enhanced student support
6. Developing stronger connections with employers
7. Growing and sustaining the programs.

Many of the challenges institutions faced were due to a lack of familiarity with these programs on the part of federal and regional regulators and institutional staff, and these are issues that may be overcome with experience and information. However, other problems were attributed by administrators to deeper issues, such as incompatibility with institutional culture. These challenges will require continued attention.

The experiences offer some lessons learned for other institutions that might be interested in developing competency-based programs. Below we summarize some key lessons learned from our discussions with Texas institutions and the literature on competency-based education.

1. Invest time and resources to ensure an adequate understanding of competency-based programs and buy-in among key stakeholders (e.g., faculty, administrative staff).
2. Leverage resources, such as existing course materials, employer input, and industry standards, to define competencies and develop resources.
3. Target students who are most likely to be successful in the non-standard structure of competency-based programs and inform students about the unique aspects of the program.
4. Enhance student tracking and support systems.
5. Continuously assess the program to ensure it is effective and sustainable and to ensure continuous improvement.

Directions for Policy and Research

In addition to the specific lessons learned that can be used by institutions to develop competency-based programs, we recommend that institutional-, state-, and federal-level policy aimed at supporting competency-based education take into consideration academic policies (e.g., transfer policies, semester credit limits), financial-aid procedures, admissions procedures, tuition structures, and business processes and practices. Further guidance to higher-education accrediting bodies would also be useful in supporting the expansion of competency-based education.

Despite a growing body of research, there are many aspects of competency-based education that require additional examination. We suggest that future research focus on the effectiveness of these programs, as well as their efficiency and sustainability. Additional research on lessons learned and best practices could help to improve the design and implementation of these programs. The impacts of competency-based programs on costs to students and institutions, as well as the systemic impacts of these programs on the cost and structure of higher education, should be explored.

Acknowledgments

The authors would like to thank the College for All Texans Foundation, the Texas Higher Education Coordinating Board, the Lumina Foundation, and the U.S. Department of Education's Institute of Education Sciences for their support of the work leading to this report. We benefited from the guidance and oversight of Nina Wright at the College for All Texans Foundation throughout the project. We appreciate the time and information provided to us by administrators at the institutions we profiled, including Western Governors University, Texas A&M Commerce, South Texas College, Texas State Technical College, Austin Community College, and Lone Star College. We thank Chandra Garber for her assistance with the organization of the document. Finally, we thank Catherine Augustine, Ann Person, and Matthew Lewis for their valuable feedback in reviewing the document. The authors alone are responsible for any errors within.

CHAPTER ONE

Introduction

A Call for Innovative Approaches to Higher Education to Improve Quality and Cut Costs

In recent years, the White House and other key stakeholders have raised concerns about the state of higher education (Hart Research Associates, 2010; Lumina Foundation, 2013; White House, 2013). In recent years, only 59 percent of university enrollees completed a bachelor's degree within six years, and only 29 percent of community college enrollees completed a degree or certificate within three years (U.S. Department of Education, 2015). The White House cites challenges with cost and quality and has called for innovative approaches to address these concerns (White House, 2013). Nonprofit organizations, such as the Lumina Foundation and the Bill & Melinda Gates Foundation, have also focused attention and funding on efforts to explore new approaches to higher education (Lumina Foundation, 2013). To address the low success rates of college enrollees and the growing costs of education, states and institutions have a wide range of efforts underway, including new technology-based tools and courses to enhance student support, financial aid, improvements to instructional content and delivery, and increased alignment and articulation between two- and four-year institutions.

A 2011 study completed by Pew Research reported that 57 percent of Americans believed that higher education fails to provide a good value for the money that students and families spend (Pew Research Center, 2011). Between 2009 and 2014, the cost of tuition, fees, and room and board for a public university in the United States increased by 17 percent, even when controlling for inflation (Baum and Ma, 2014). Public financial aid has also been increasing (College Board, 2014), resulting in the burden of rising college costs falling on taxpayers as well as students and families. And yet, despite increases in financial aid, the rising cost of college remains a significant barrier to college access and success for many potential enrollees (Long, 2014, and Nagaoka, Roderick, and Coca, 2009). To address the rising cost of college, the White House has proposed a number of different approaches, including paying institutions based on their performance, continuing to increase federal financial aid, and providing free access to community college for all students (White House, 2013 and 2015).

President Obama has emphasized workforce readiness "for the jobs of today and tomorrow" as a primary goal for higher education (White House, 2013). Yet evidence also indicates skill mismatch with workforce needs. In a 2010 survey administered on behalf of the Association of American Colleges and Universities, one-third of employers reported that higher education was not sufficiently preparing students for entry-level positions (Hart Research Associates, 2010). Studies indicate that students who graduate from certain institutions and major fields face significant challenges in obtaining employment after graduation, and returns in the form of higher salaries may be elusive for many (Belfield, Liu, and Trimble, 2014; Carnevale, Cheah, and Hanson, 2015; Deming, Goldin, and Katz, 2011). Employers argue that there needs to be a greater focus in higher education on learning outcomes to ensure that graduates are obtaining the knowledge, skills, and abilities necessary to move directly into the workforce (Hart Research Associates, 2010). There is a range of different efforts underway to improve the match between graduates and employers. For example, the White House now provides the College Scorecard that allows students to compare employment rates for graduates across schools (White House, 2014). Some states, including Texas, require institutions to consult with employer advisory boards when creating vocational degree and certificate programs.

The Rise of Competency-Based Education

Competency-based education has risen as one potential solution to the concerns about the cost of higher education and the ability of students to complete degree and certificate programs. Although there is no single definition of competency-based education in the literature, most agree on at least one central feature: competency-based education focuses on what a student is expected to know and be able to do at the end of the program (i.e., "competencies") and awards degrees or certificates solely on student mastery of these competencies (Bell and Conklin, 2013; Person, Goble and Bruch, 2014; Porter and Reilly, 2014). With mastery of competencies as the sole determinant of completion, these programs often allow for variation in the time it takes for students to move through coursework, as well as variation in the approach to mastering competencies. Such an approach aligns with several of the innovative strategies supported by the President, including the call for credits to be awarded according to learning rather than seat time and for the use of technology to redesign courses and provide student support (White House, 2013). Institutions with competency-based programs—such as Western Governors University (WGU) and Southern New Hampshire University—have been referenced by the White House as models for innovation.

While the past decade has seen particular momentum for the competency-based education movement, competency-based education has held a place in U.S. higher education for nearly 50 years. Klein-Collins (2012) traces the birth of competency-based education in higher education to the 1960s, when the government funded ten higher-education institutions to develop teacher training programs. These programs included many of the features that are common to competency-based programs today, including a curriculum based on competencies, personalization, and a focus on assessment. Other fields, such as medicine and nursing, have also had a long history of competency-based approaches to education (Klein-Collins, 2012). The federal government's Fund for the Improvement of Postsecondary Education provided financial support for adult learning programs to develop competency-based approaches (Klein-Collins, 2013). These programs laid the groundwork for the competency-based programs in development today.

In recent years, the government has moved to reduce barriers to expansion for competency-based degree programs. In 2005, the government amended the Higher Education Act of 1965 to allow direct-assessment programs—programs that move completely away from credit hours and courses—to be accepted into the federal financial-aid programs.[1] In addition, the U.S. Department of Education set out in 2009 to revise the definition of the credit hour. According to the Department of Education, the revised definition "does not emphasize the concept of 'seat time' (time in class) as the primary metric" (Ochoa, 2011, and Silva, White, and Toch, 2015). In 2013, a variety of stakeholders, including the White House, the Department of Education, higher-education institutions, the Council for Higher Education Accreditation, and several state higher-education officers, met to discuss competency-based education and attempt to build consensus around efforts to expand it in higher education (Klein-Collins, 2013). These efforts have helped to provide a more-supportive environment for the development of competency-based programs.

Documenting the Landscape for Competency-Based Higher Education in Texas

The purpose of this report is to describe existing competency-based degree and certificate programs in Texas and to place these efforts within the context of the national literature on competency-based programs in higher education. We describe the six higher-education institutions that currently have competency-based programs in place in Texas: Austin Community College (ACC),

---

[1]   Direct-assessment programs are distinct from course-based programs. Course-based programs map competencies onto courses with credit-hour equivalents and develop programs with a full 120 credits, so administratively students look similar to students in traditional programs. Direct-assessments programs only map assessments to competencies, so they face stricter scrutiny by accreditors and additional layers of administrative barriers with regard to issues, such as financial aid and transfer of credits. See U.S. Congress, 2006.

Lone Star College, South Texas College (STC), Texas A&M Commerce (TAMUC), Texas State Technical College (TSTC), and WGU. From the experiences of these institutions and the competency-based education literature, we draw some lessons. In addition, we discuss possible research and policy options that could help determine whether these programs do in fact offer high-quality pathways for students and what would facilitate the growth of high-quality degree and certificate programs.

Our approach to the report relied primarily on three methods: a search of the existing literature on competency-based programs in higher education, interviews conducted in fall 2014 with a variety of stakeholders in Texas, and a review of Texas program documentation.

To conduct the literature review, we started with the resources provided online by organizations that have gathered research on competency-based education (e.g., Lumina Foundation); we also conducted a broader search of online resources using search terms such as "competency based" and "higher education." While there are a number of resources on competency-based approaches in the K–12 education literature and workforce-training literature, we limited the scope of our literature review to resources that focus specifically on higher education.

Our interviewees included administrators at institutions that offer competency-based degree or certificate programs (nine interviewees across the six institutions), students who are currently enrolled in competency-based degree programs (nine interviews at one institution), and a staff member at the Texas Higher Education Coordinating Board (THECB). Instruments for our administrator and student interviews are included in the Appendix. Contact information for administrators was provided by THECB staff, and all administrators we contacted agreed to participate. The students we interviewed were drawn from all current enrollees at one of the six Texas institutions we studied. The program director provided contact information for all current enrollees, and we emailed all students with the offer of a $25 incentive to participate in a one-hour interview. The first nine students to volunteer were chosen to be interviewees. To supplement the interviews, we reviewed available documentation on each program. We searched program websites, drew from studies in the literature, and asked our interviewees to send relevant documentation.

Limitations of the Study

There are some strong limitations to the methods used for this study. Descriptions of existing competency-based degree programs are based largely on self-reported data by our interviewees, and in many cases we did not have other sources to validate administrator interview data. In addition, we did not account for the perspectives of other important stakeholders that may play a role in competency-based education, such as faculty, accreditors, and financial-aid administrators. Interviews with students are limited to just one institution and therefore do not generalize to student experiences in Texas competency-based education programs. In addition, students volunteered to be interviewed rather than being selected at random, so they may not be representative of student experiences in the institution. Analysis of interview data, however, elicited a shared set of themes across respondents, and these themes are echoed in a prior study of student experiences in programs in other states (Klein-Collins and Baylor, 2013), suggesting that there may be some common experiences for students in Texas programs and students in programs that are documented elsewhere in the literature.

Report Overview

In Chapter Two, we provide a description of the key elements of competency-based education and the various models of competency-based education that exist in U.S. higher education. We describe the potential benefits of this model, concerns about it, and existing evidence in the literature on lessons learned and best practices. In Chapter Three, we use administrator interviews and a review of program documentation to describe the competency-based degree or certificate programs at each of the six institutions offering them in Texas. We also describe the experiences of students in one program. Finally, in Chapter Four, we draw from the literature and our interview data to identify potential next steps for Texas state policymakers and institutional leaders to consider. These include research to determine whether competency-based programs are effective and how they can be improved, and policy changes to facilitate the growth of high-quality programs in the case they are found to be effective.

CHAPTER TWO

Understanding Competency-Based Education Programs

Key Features of Competency-Based Education Programs

As described above, competency-based education centers on competencies—the knowledge and skills that a student is expected to have after completing a program. According to Klein-Collins (2012), there are two ways that institutions incorporate competency-based frameworks into higher education. The first approach is to integrate competency frameworks into existing traditional programs with semester-length courses. For example, some faculty members have adopted a competency-based approach to curriculum design, determining the necessary knowledge, skills, and abilities that students should have by the end of the course and aligning course content and assessments with these competencies. In many cases, these faculty members have also moved toward assessing students through portfolios that provide a range of evidence demonstrating mastery of competencies; they may see these as more effective than traditional assessments for gauging knowledge, skills, and abilities in applied settings. These programs, however, often retain a common course length and continue to place the instructor as the central figure in driving student learning. In addition, while individual courses may be designed around competencies, the full degrees and certificates are not often mapped to competencies in traditional degree and certificate programs.

Another method of integrating a competency-based approach into traditional course-based programs allows students to obtain credit for earlier learning—e.g., from job training, military experience, and prior coursework—by administering a prior-learning assessment. These prior-learning assessments can include both portfolio assessments, such as those administered by the Council for Adult and Experiential Learning (CAEL), and standardized tests, such as the College Level Examination Program. For remaining coursework, programs may retain a traditional structure centered on seat time (time in class), with traditional curricula and instructor-driven learning. While such programs adopt a feature of competency-based education into the existing program, they do not use competency-based approaches to fully reform the approach to education.

This paper focuses on a different, whole-program approach to competency-based education, in which competencies are used as a means to drive curricular redesign and move away from seat-time requirements (Klein-Collins, 2012). These approaches map a clear set of competencies across all coursework within a program and allow students to progress through a program at their own pace, based on demonstrating mastery of competencies through a range of assessments. Many agree that the ability of programs to decouple education from seat time and to allow students to complete degrees at a variable pace is an essential element of competency-based programs (Bell, 2013; Johnstone and Soares, 2014; Klein-Collins, 2013; Person, Goble, and Bruch, 2014).

While two features are viewed as central to these competency-based education programs—curricular design around competencies and the ability of individuals to move through coursework at variable paces—other features of competency-based higher education vary somewhat from program to program and institution to institution. Below we describe some of these areas of variation, including the structure of the program, the content and delivery, the roles of faculty and support staff, and the tuition structure. A description of the business-management bachelor's program at WGU is provided in Box 2.1 as an example of a competency-based degree program.

Program Scope: As Porter and Reilly (2014) describe, institutions have taken varied approaches to building the institutional structure around their competency-based programs. Some institutions have chosen to transform existing programs or develop new pro-

Box 2.1
Sample Requirements for a Competency-Based Program

Bachelor of Science in Business Management
Western Governors University

Program Requirements
Students must complete 30 courses and a capstone project. Completion of a course is determined by passing all relevant assessments; passing an assessment means students have demonstrated competency equivalent to a B grade (80 percent) or better.

Course and Project Requirements
- *General education:* English Composition I and II; Foundations of College Mathematics; College Algebra; Introduction to Probability and Statistics; Introduction to Geography; Introduction to Humanities; Integrated Natural Science; Integrated Natural Science and Applications; Critical Thinking and Logic; Elements of Effective Communication
- *Leadership and management:* Organizational Behavior and Leadership; Principles of Management
- *Business law and ethics:* Fundamentals of Business Law and Ethics; Legal Issues for Business Organizations; Ethical Situations in Business
- *Accounting:* Principles of Accounting; Managerial Accounting
- *Economics:* Microeconomics; Macroeconomics; Global Business
- *Marketing and communication:* Fundamentals of Marketing and Business Communication; Marketing Applications
- *Business management:* Strategy, Change and Organizational Behavior Concepts; Quality, Operations, and Decision Science Concepts; Business Management Tasks
- *Other courses:* Finance, Quantitative Analysis for Business, Information Systems Management, Project Management
- Business Management Capstone Written Project

Sample Competencies (Business Management Tasks Course)*
- The graduate explains appropriate quality management strategies for continuous improvement in an organization.
- The graduate analyzes forecasting models, measurement techniques, and scheduling methods.
- The graduate describes different innovation strategies and the role leaders play in innovation.
- The graduate describes the role of teams in organizational effectiveness and the influence of individual behavior on team dynamics.

*NOTE: These are new competencies planned to be in place January 2016.

grams on a program-by-program basis, with the program integrated into the institution alongside traditional degree programs. This allows institutions to demonstrate the benefits of competency-based education on a smaller scale before expanding to other programs. In addition, these institutions can provide such options as separate tracks that are targeted to competency-based certificate/degree programs and certain types of students. On the other end of the spectrum, institutions such as WGU are designed entirely around a competency-based framework, allowing the institution to design systems specific to the needs of competency-based programs (e.g., administration, assessment, technology) and hire staff to focus exclusively on competency-based programs. Another option is to open a separate unit of the institution to house the competency-based programs, given their unique structure and administrative requirements.

Program Type: A common distinction in competency-based education is whether the program is considered "direct assessment" or "course based." According to the Southern Association of Colleges and Schools Commission on Colleges (SACSCOC), the regional accreditor for Texas colleges:

> Federal regulations define a direct assessment competency-based educational program as an instructional program that, in lieu of credit hours or clock hours as a measure of student learning, uses direct assessment of student learning relying solely on the attainment of defined competencies, or recognizes the direct assessment of student learning by others. (SACSCOC, 2013)

In practice, course-based programs look similar to direct-assessment programs across most characteristics, including the use of assessments to measure learning, the tying of assessments to competencies, and allowing students to move through the competencies at variable paces. The key distinction is that competency-based programs labeled as "direct assessment" abandon the use of credit hours and courses and focus entirely on the competencies and their related assessments to structure the degree program (Fain, 2014, and Book, 2014). Examples of institutions with direct assessment programs include Southern New Hampshire University and Capella University. The direct-assessment approach to competency-based education has been less prevalent, as the move away from credit hours creates substantial challenges for institutions around accreditation, financial aid, transfer of students to other institutions, and institutional data systems and processes (Book, 2014).

Calendar Design and Course-Taking Requirements: To facilitate self-paced learning, the literature suggests that academic calendars be flexible and continuous and that learning materials be continuously accessible to students (Bell and Conklin, 2013, and Johnstone and Soares, 2014). Institutions have taken varying approaches to modifying calendar design. Some programs, such as those at WGU, offer a fixed term length and allow students to complete as many courses as desired during that fixed term. Students can complete and enroll in new courses at any time. Others use a more structured approach of offering multiple lengths of terms for courses (i.e., 14 week, 12 week, 10 week, seven week). These institutions also allow students to complete courses at any time within the term, but students can only enroll in new courses when a new variable-length term begins. Many institutions set requirements for the number of courses that can be taken at one time to ensure that students are not overextended. In some courses there may be regularly structured course activities or a suggested pacing guide to ensure that students are completing coursework in a timely fashion, but participation in these activities and compliance with suggested pacing is typically not required, as this would hinder students from advancing more quickly.

Faculty Roles: An important aspect of many competency-based programs is the shift from an instructor-centered education model to a student-centered model (Klein-Collins, 2013, and Ordonez, 2014). In the student-centered model, instructors act as coaches and mentors for students. They set expectations for what should be learned, help direct students to materials they might access to build knowledge in certain areas, and address student questions as they arise. This stands in contrast to traditional programs, in which instructors may spend much of their time lecturing, may prescribe a common set of materials, and may require students to complete assignments throughout the term in addition to final assessments. Some schools, such as WGU, have completely overhauled the role of faculty and other staff members to allow them to focus on their specific role in their competency-based programs (Person, Goble, and Bruch, 2014). Program staff are hired into one of a number of tracks: curriculum development, assessment design, course material selection, tutoring/direct instruction, student academic support, and the grading of student assessments. Other competency-based programs, however, continue to require a single faculty member to play multiple roles. Institutions also vary in their decisions around staffing: some draw on existing faculty, while others bring in new faculty; some ask faculty to teach traditional and competency-based courses, others bring in faculty to focus solely on the competency-based program.

Student Supports: Competency-based programs often provide additional student supports beyond what students have access to in traditional degree programs. The programs require students to take the initiative in driving learning and provide substantial autonomy as they move through courses, so many consider stronger student support services essential (Klein-Collins and Baylor, 2013). Many institutions hire new staff (often referred to as *coaches*) who are assigned to and provide support for students throughout their time in the program. While academic instructors are responsible for specific content-related support for a particular course, coaches provide more general support throughout the program for academic and nonacademic issues. These coaches can help students stay motivated, ensure that students get the assistance they need from instructors and tutors in order to master the material, and offer students guidance as they choose courses and work through what is for many an unfamiliar pathway. To ensure that students are staying on track, instructors and/or coaches may use real-time data on student use of online resources to track student progress in accessing materials and completing assessments, intervening as needed (Johnstone and Soares, 2014). Online-learning management systems that track student progress can be particularly helpful in supporting such student monitoring. Data collected on students' access of materials can be used to run statistical models that identify predictors of student success (Ordonez, 2014).

Instructional Mode: Competency-based programs are primarily delivered online (Klein-Collins, 2013, and Book, 2014), but some either require or offer face-to-face instruction as well. Institutions commonly house materials on a learning-management system, and students interact with instructors through a range of methods, including email, phone, web meeting, and in-person components. Some programs may also require participation in face-to-face components with the full class or with the instructor. For example, some aspects of the program may be "hands on," requiring instructors to demonstrate skills to students in person and monitor students as they practice the skills. Other programs may simply make face-to-face opportunities, such as labs or office hours, available as a means of support.

Program Content: There is substantial variation in the curriculum materials used across competency-based programs. Some programs rely primarily on structured modules that are vendor or instructor designed, while others encourage students to draw from a range of different types of materials (e.g., videos, articles, resources in current work settings) to build knowledge and skills around a particular competency (Klein-Collins and Baylor, 2013). Most importantly, as described above, the student typically plays a more central role in determining what information is accessed. Even within the same program, students may vary in the curriculum materials they access, both because students enter the program with differing knowledge and skill sets, and because students may learn best in different ways and may therefore choose their preferred resources (Johnstone and Soares, 2014). This approach to education is often referred to as personalized or individualized learning. In addition to the personalized nature of many competency-based education programs, these programs are often offered in applied fields (e.g., IT, leadership and management), and the material in these programs often tends to be more applied.

Assessments: Given that competency-based education aims to ensure a common set of knowledge, skills, and abilities among those who complete the programs, assessments play a central role in ensuring that graduates have met these standards. Competency-based programs often use a range of assessment types within a single program or course, including computerized exams, projects, essays, research papers, problem solving, and demonstrations (Klein-Collins and Baylor, 2013). In addition, competency-based programs often provide opportunities for students to take a pretest to gauge their incoming knowledge, skills, and abilities. The results of this assessment can be used to guide students and instructors to the areas where a student needs additional development and the content the student should focus on. Many competency-based programs will allow students who achieve high scores on a pretest to move directly to the final assessment, given that they may already have mastered the material. Some argue that the security of these assessments is critical given their central role in assuring high-quality graduates (Johnstone and Soares, 2014). As a result, many competency-based programs continue to require assessments to be proctored in person or electronically.

Tuition Structure: In addition to moving away from traditional course structures, some competency-based programs have made attempts to move away from traditional tuition structures. These institutions have implemented a subscription-based model in which students pay a fixed price for a term and are able to master as many competencies and complete as many courses as they can during that term. By decoupling tuition from seat time, these institutions allow students to potentially save both time and money by moving through coursework quickly (Porter and Reilly, 2014). On the other hand, there can be significant legal, regulatory, and procedural barriers to altering tuition structures and that may deter experimentation.

The Potential Benefits of Competency-Based Higher Education

Competency-based higher education is thought to have a range of potential benefits for students, institutions, and employers. With respect to employers, the use of competencies to structure programs might ensure that students are being trained more directly for their roles in the workplace, particularly if employers play a role in defining competencies (Bergeron, 2013). Some argue that degrees, majors, and course names from traditional programs provide comparatively weak signals for employers on the knowledge, skills, and abilities that an individual has obtained through higher education. Employers can benefit from the "improved signal" that competency-based programs provide, where employers can learn exactly what skills and abilities a student has mastered based on the equivocal description of those skills acquired in competency-based programs. This is facilitated by standard requirements for mastery across all students and the fact that competencies are often clearly laid out on a student's transcript (Bergeron, 2013). Graduates can then be matched to jobs according to exactly what they know and are able to do (i.e., competencies) rather than major fields, which tend to be only for a rough proxy for competencies (Bergeron, 2013).

Competency-based programs also provide a pathway for students who may not succeed in traditional programs. Students may benefit from the self-paced nature of the instruction, as it increases their flexibility to complete the work around other obligations, and the individualized nature of instruction may help them to stay motivated and focused (Bell, 2013; Johnstone and Soares, 2014; Ordonez, 2014). This may be particularly important for nontraditional students, that is, older students who often have jobs, families, and other life obligations that prevent them from being able to attend traditional courses. Students who can move through the material more quickly are also able to finish the degree or certificate in a shorter time, and a quicker time to degree increases the likelihood that students will finish a program (Complete College America, 2011). The ability to receive credit for prior experience and education also shortens the time to degree, potentially saving students time and money, and increasing the likelihood of success (Porter and Reilly, 2014). The benefit is likely to be particularly great for nontraditional students who may have already mastered some of the required competencies from years of work, military experience, or prior time in college. For students who attend institutions that offer subscription fees to separate tuition from seat time and students who are able to pretest out of coursework based on prior experience, the potential lower cost of competency-based programs may also be a substantial benefit (Porter and Reilly, 2014).

While the most substantial benefits of competency-based education are likely to be experienced by employers and students, institutions can also benefit from the programs. These programs offer new pathways that are particularly attractive to nontraditional students, so they may draw new students who would not otherwise choose to pursue a degree or certificate, thus increasing enrollment. In addition, institutions can better ensure that their graduates leave with a set of skills and abilities expected by employers. This could potentially help students move more seamlessly into employment (assuming that the competencies are aligned with employer needs), leading to higher employment rates, a potentially important measure of institutional quality (Klein-Collins, 2012).

It is unclear whether competency-based degree programs are less expensive to implement than traditional programs (Porter and Reilly, 2014). Institutions tend to experience large start-up costs for competency-based programs. Although the per-student costs may be somewhat lower (particularly for online programs), it may take many years for institutions to recover start-up costs (Porter and Reilly, 2014). Advocates of competency-based programs hypothesize that cost savings will eventually be realized as programs mature.

Concerns About Competency-Based Higher Education

While advocates of competency-based education tout its potential benefits, others express concerns. Some argue that competency-based programs are not of equivalent quality to traditional education. The applied nature of many of the programs raises concerns that students will lose the ability to relate skills to underlying theory and to apply competencies across varied settings (Mitchell and Bell, 2000). In addition, critics worry that asking a student to demonstrate a skill does not ensure that the student has the knowledge and understanding of the surrounding context (O'Donoghue and Chapman, 2010). A related concern is that the modular nature of the content will reduce opportunities for students to make connections across different competencies (O'Donoghue and Chapman, 2010). Those who are concerned about the quality of competency-based education also cite the reduced level of interaction, both between instructors and students and between students and their peers (O'Donoghue and Chapman, 2010). The development of social skills, such as teamwork and collaboration, are considered by many to be an important component of higher education, and to the degree that online, self-paced programs are limited in their ability to provide these skills, they may be of potentially lower quality. As documented in a recent *Time* article, some fear that competency-based programs will become degree mills, setting questionable standards and producing large numbers of graduates without the skills needed to be successful in the workforce (Krupnick, 2015).

There are also concerns about the systemic impacts of competency-based programs. Critics fear that the introduction of these programs will result in a two-tier system of education, where more advantaged students are able to enroll in higher-quality traditional programs while disadvantaged students are relegated to low-quality competency-based programs (Porter and Reilly, 2014). There are also concerns that competency-based programs will cannibalize students and revenues from traditional programs (HCM Strategists, 2013). In addition, as the role of the instructor shifts away from being central to the delivery of content, fewer faculty members may be needed, and this may lead to job loss for many who currently hold these positions (Shapiro, 2014).

Existing Research on Competency-Based Higher Education Programs

The body of literature on competency-based programs in higher education has been growing in recent years, with a number of papers that attempt to define competency-based education, describe particular competency-based institutions and programs, document the benefits and limitations of competency-based education, and offer some lessons learned. For example, a consulting firm provides a fact sheet on competency-based education (Bell, 2013). A number of studies have examined existing programs to identify lessons learned (Book, 2014; Council for Adult and Experiential Learning, 2014; HCM Strategists, 2013; Person, Goble, and Bruch, 2014). In addition, some of the papers focus on challenges that the competency-based movement faces and call for policy changes that could help overcome these barriers. For example, Bell and Conklin (2013) examine the issue of state financial aid and the varying barriers that competency-based programs face, depending on particular state laws and policies.

Despite a growing body of literature on competency-based education, the studies have largely been descriptive historical accounts or white papers advocating for particular policy changes. There have been no rigorous studies to compare the impacts of various models of education on student outcomes, costs, and other impacts of these programs. While studies of implementation and the perspectives of key stakeholders (such as this one) can offer institutions some "lessons" about how best to avoid challenges, there are no studies that can offer a research-based guide on best practices for competency-based degree and certificate programs or provide compelling evidence about the impact of competency-based programs on students.

While this paper contributes to the descriptive literature on competency-based programs, we are unable to rigorously assess the quality and effectiveness of these programs. Therefore, we conclude this paper with a potential research agenda and set of policy considerations that could help to assess the value of competency-based programs and support the development of high-quality competency-based programs.

CHAPTER THREE

Competency-Based Degree and Certificate Programs in Texas

In this chapter, we describe the current landscape for competency-based higher education in Texas. We spoke with administrators at each of the six institutions offering competency-based degree programs in Texas, reviewed relevant websites and program documentation where available, and in some cases found literature describing the programs that could be used to supplement our primary data collection. In addition to speaking with representatives of the institutions, we interviewed THECB staff involved in the development of competency-based programs and students in one of the competency-based programs.

Existing Competency-Based Degree and Certificate Programs

Texas has many higher-education institutions that incorporate some aspects of competency-based education, but have not fully restructured their programs to be competency based. For example, as we have learned from our THECB interviews, many faculty members at institutions across Texas structure courses around learning outcomes or competencies. Success in most of these courses, however, requires participation for the full term, and in many cases, courses are largely lecture based, with the instructor playing the central role in driving learning as students progress together as a cohort. And while courses may be designed according to learning outcomes, the degree and certificate programs, as a whole, are not necessarily mapped to competencies. As another example of incorporating a competency-based feature into traditional programs, some programs (e.g., bachelor of applied arts and science programs) provide opportunities for students to obtain credit for prior knowledge and skills gained through work experience by successfully completing assessments given upon enrollment. After being given credit for prior experience and knowledge, however, students enroll in traditional lecture-based coursework for the remainder of the program.

For the purposes of this study, we are focusing on programs that use a competency-based approach to restructure a full degree or certificate program and decouple degree completion from seat time. As of fall 2014, these accredited competency-based programs existed at six higher-education institutions in Texas, including two universities, three community colleges, and a technical college. These institutions vary across a range of characteristics. We provide a description of each program below, and a summary of the programs in Table 3.1.

Competency-based programs generally attract nontraditional populations, and administrators reported that individuals with work and/or school experience and those who are currently working have found the greatest success in the programs. They reported that many of the students are those who have much of the knowledge, experience, and training required to meet the competencies associated with a degree program, but this knowledge has not been leveraged to complete a degree. Administrators believe that younger students do not do well in the programs because they do not have prior experience with navigating education- or work-related environments autonomously. Some respondents reported that their institutions require students to have prior college experience before entering to ensure that they are bringing in the types of students who are most likely to succeed in the self-paced, student-driven environment that characterizes their competency-based programs. The exception to this among Texas programs is TSTC; only a quarter of students in the TSTC programs are adult learners.

The following program descriptions highlight some of the key aspects of each program, including the field and type of program, the delivery of instruction and faculty roles, the design and use of program content and assessments, and the structure of tuition.

Western Governors University

Degree Type and Program Scope: WGU is a private, nonprofit institution built entirely around competency-based degree programs. As one of the first institutions in the United States to move away from seat time and instead rely primarily on assessment as a means of moving through degree requirements, it is seen by many as a model for competency-based education. The university was developed by the request of the Western Governors Association, an association of the governors in 19 states, and began providing degree programs to students across the nation in 1998. After looking at the landscape for higher education in the 1990s, the governors decided that an alternative model was necessary to meet the needs of nontraditional learners and to meet workforce needs in the states while leveraging the possibilities associated with online education. WGU was designed to offer programs in four areas: teacher education, business, IT, and health professions. The level of the programs ranges from teaching licensure to bachelor's and master's degrees.

Faculty Roles and Delivery of Instruction: The vast majority of the institution's coursework is provided online, though several of the programs require small in-person components (e.g., nursing, teacher education). WGU has taken a unique approach to reforming faculty roles, dividing the roles that are traditionally played by a single faculty member into different specialty tracks into which individuals are hired: curriculum development, assessment design, course material selection, tutoring/direct instruction, student academic support, and the grading of student assessments (Person, Goble, and Bruch, 2014). Students initially meet with faculty mentors once a week by phone and, according to needs, these calls may shift to biweekly as the student progresses. Faculty mentors use a variety of electronic methods to interact with students. Students play a central role, however, in driving the learning process, accessing resources at their own pace, and completing assessments when they (and their faculty mentor) agree they have mastered all of the competencies in a particular course.

Table 3.1
Description of Basic Program Characteristics

Institution	Degree Program(s)	Program Scope	Program Type	Percentage of Adult Learners	Faculty Roles	Delivery of Instruction	Calendar Structure	Tuition Structure
Western Governors University	Teachers college, business, IT, health professions (all levels)	Whole institution	Course based	95%	Specialized faculty tracks, including curriculum development, assessment design, course material selection, tutoring/direct course instruction, student academic advising/support, and the grading of student assessments	Online	Six month	Subscription ($3,000/term)
Texas A&M Commerce	Bachelor of Applied Arts and Sciences (BAAS), Organizational Leadership	Standalone program	Course based	95%	Instructor responsible for content design, course instruction, academic support, assessments grading; coaches provide other support	Online	Seven week	Subscription ($750/term)
South Texas College	Bachelor of Applied Science (BAS), Organizational Leadership	Standalone program	Course based	90%	Instructor responsible for content design, course instruction, academic support, assessments grading; coaches provide other support	Online and in-person reqs	Seven week	Subscription ($750/term)

Table 3.1—Continued

Institution	Degree Program(s)	Program Scope	Program Type	Percentage of Adult Learners	Faculty Roles	Delivery of Instruction	Calendar Structure	Tuition Structure
Texas State Technical College	Level 1 Certificates, Industrial Systems Techn. and Industrial Maint. Mechanic	Two separate, standalone programs	Direct assessment	60%	Instructor responsible for content design, course instruction, academic support, assessments grading; coaches provide other support	Online and in-person reqs	Eight week	Subscription ($200–300/term)
Austin Community College (ACC)	Certificate, Accelerated Programmer Training	Several associated programs grouped together	Course based	95%	Instructor responsible for content design, course instruction, academic support, assessments grading; coaches provide other support	Online	16-week, 12-week, eight-week	Credit-hour based ($80/credit)
Lone Star College	Certificate, Accelerated IT Program; Accelerated Business 2+2 Program	Standalone program	Course based	Not available	Instructor responsible for content design, course instruction, academic support, assessments grading; coaches provide other support	Online	16 week, 12 week, eight week	Credit-hour based ($80/credit)

Program Content and Assessments: Program competencies are set by external councils made up of employers and academic experts from other universities. Once set, courses are created that reflect those competencies and ensure a student masters them by the time he/she graduates. Assessments at the course level are developed by a team of psychometricians and academic experts. These take many forms from online tests, research papers, demonstrations, and the like. Students' performance assessments are evaluated by a separate set of faculty (not those who support the students' learning activities). Students pass an assessment by scoring at least a B (as set by the grading rubrics used by the evaluators). Many of the courses also have pretests to allow students to gauge how to spend their study time. If a student and his/her faculty member agree the performance on a pretest is sufficiently strong, the student may sit for the final proctored assessment. All students in the same programs take the same courses; there are no electives.

Tuition Structure: WGU offers its programs in six-month terms; students are able to take as many courses as they are able to complete during that time. Most students take courses one at a time and move on to a new course when they have completed the previous one. The tuition and fees for a six-month term are approximately $3,000.

Texas A&M University Commerce

Degree Type and Program Scope: TAMUC currently offers one competency-based degree program, a Bachelor of Applied Arts and Sciences in Organizational Leadership. As we will describe later in this chapter, the program was developed through a grant awarded by the EDUCAUSE Next Generation Learning Challenge.[1] The institution decided to offer the program because of their commitment to serv-

---

[1] EDUCAUSE is a nonprofit organization made up of institutions of higher education, corporations serving the higher education IT market, and other related associations and organizations. Its members contribute to thought leadership on major issues, help clarify the current environment, document effective practices, and highlight how emerging trends and technologies may influence the evolution of IT in higher education. The Next Generation Learning Challenges is a collaboration to address the barriers to educational innovation by tapping the potential of technology to improve college readiness and completion, particularly for low-income young adults.

ing adult learners and other nontraditional students, as well as a desire to develop more innovative programs. Our interviewees reported that Organizational Leadership is a desirable field for a competency-based degree program because it provides nontraditional students an opportunity to acquire and demonstrate competencies that are essential for career advancement in many fields. In the future, the institution would like to offer a competency-based leadership program that is specific to criminal justice.

Faculty Roles, Delivery of Instruction, and Student Supports: The Organizational Leadership program at TAMUC is delivered entirely online. Materials and assessments are delivered through a learning-management system. Instructors act as facilitators of the learning process, using the results of the pretest to guide the learning path for each student. Instructors primarily communicate with students through email, with emails to the full cohort of students enrolled in a course, as well as to individual students. In addition to instructors, students are provided with an individual success coach who works in an advisory capacity to address issues related to academic achievement or personal challenges to ensure progress through learning modules. Communication between students and success coaches takes place by phone and email, typically outside of the learning-management system.

Program Content and Assessments: TAMUC did not have a traditional degree program in Organizational Leadership when the competency-based program was developed, so they could not directly map the program to existing courses. As we will describe in a later section, these competencies were identified jointly with the THECB and STC with the help of advisory committees made up of a range of stakeholders, including faculty and industry representatives. These competencies were used to develop courses that comprise the new degree program. The general-education courses must adhere to particular parameters from the state because they are transferrable courses; the upper-division courses allowed for greater flexibility. Upon enrollment in a course, students first take a pretest, and if they score an 80 or above on the pretest, they are able to move directly to a post-test. If the students also receive an 80 or above on the posttest, they are recognized as having mastered the competency and are given credit for the coursework. For competencies that have not been previously mastered, students have access to a variety of resources on a learning-management system that can be used to build knowledge, skills, and abilities. While lower-division courses are primarily assessed through testing, upper-division courses often require students to demonstrate mastery of competencies through projects and other course materials that are submitted through an online portfolio. Even in the lower-division courses, the tests are not necessarily multiple-choice tests; many require students to write essays and demonstrate knowledge through practical applications.

Tuition Structure: Students in TAMUC's Organizational Leadership program pay for the program through a subscription model at a cost of $750 for a seven-week term, during which they are able to complete as many credits as they are able. Students typically enroll in two courses per term, but some students have been able to complete as many as nine courses in a single term.

South Texas College

Degree Type and Program Scope: There are many similarities between the STC and TAMUC programs, as these programs were developed through a collaborative EDUCAUSE grant. We describe partnership efforts between the institutions and the state in greater detail in the next section. STC also offers a competency-based program in Organizational Leadership, though it is classified as a bachelor of applied science. Administrators reported that the institution was selected for the program by the THECB in part because STC is a community college with authorization to grant baccalaureate degrees in applied-science fields.[2] The field of Organizational Leadership was particularly attractive because of its relevance to working adults across multiple sectors who are looking to advance their careers.

Faculty Roles, Delivery of Instruction, and Student Supports: In contrast to the TAMUC program, the STC program has been offered

---

[2]   STC is one of three institutions in Texas that was allowed to participate in a pilot study through which community colleges were granted the authority to provide applied baccalaureate programs in a limited number of areas.

as a hybrid program. The first 90 credit hours, including core courses and lower-division elective courses, are offered entirely online. Upper-division courses, on the other hand, require students to attend face-to-face courses one day each week, while the rest of the course is delivered online. In fall 2016, however, the program transitions to entirely online delivery. For the most part, communication with instructors occurs through emails or the learning-management system, and sometimes by phone or in person. Students have the opportunity to schedule in-person meetings with instructors and can also visit during regularly scheduled office hours. Students have access to a single success coach through email and phone calls, though occasionally they meet in person. The communication between students and the success coach focuses on general academic advising, helping students to overcome fears and other barriers, facilitating efforts to find the resources they need to support learning, and counseling students on plans for the future.

Program Content and Assessments: To develop the content for the program, administrators met on a monthly basis with faculty from TAMUC and STC and industry stakeholders to determine what a student should know and be able to do upon completion of a course. These advisory committees, one for general education and one for upper-division courses, developed the competencies. The demonstration of competency mastery is identical to what was described for TAMUC; students take pretests and, in the case of prior mastery, they are able to move to a posttest and, if successful, earn the credit immediately. For competencies that have not been mastered, students are provided with a variety of content that they can utilize to facilitate learning, including nongraded assignments on which they can receive feedback from instructors. Students demonstrate mastery in lower-division courses through testing that may include multiple-choice questions, essays, practical demonstration of knowledge, and other assessment strategies. Students demonstrate mastery in upper-division courses through a range of assessment types that are used to identify application of knowledge, including portfolios and projects.

Tuition Structure: The tuition structure for the STC program is identical to that for TAMUC's program, with a $750 subscription fee

for a seven-week term. Administrators reported that students traditionally take two courses per term, but a small number take just one course,
while others are able to complete three or four courses in a term.

Texas State Technical College

Degree Type and Program Scope: TSTC currently offers two
competency-based degree programs, a level-one certificate in industrial systems technology and a level-one certificate in technology
maintenance mechanics. TSTC is also in the process of developing a
competency-based framework for several other programs, including air conditioning and refrigeration, welding, and certified nursing assistance. TSTC decided to pursue competency-based education
in order to provide students with alternative ways to gain skills and
obtain degrees or certificates. Administrators learned from employers that there was a strong unmet demand for graduates of industrial
systems technology programs. Our interviewees reported that competency-based degree programs were developed to increase the number
of graduates in a short time period by giving students an opportunity
to accelerate their degree programs. As overseers of a technical college,
administrators argued that they had long focused on the specific needs
of employers to design program content. With the establishment of
competency-based programs, they redesigned full certificate programs
to ensure that they were streamlined toward mastery of specific competencies. TSTC chose to develop the programs as direct-assessment
programs that are not tied to credit hours, requiring the institution to
seek approval from the federal government for financial-aid eligibility
and to pursue a substantive change process[3] with the regional accreditor, the SACSCOC.

Faculty Roles, Delivery of Instruction, and Student Supports: The
industrial systems technology program is primarily delivered online,
though instructors occasionally require students to come into the class-
room for structured hands-on activities, and labs are open daily from

---

[3] Substantive change is a significant modification or expansion of the nature and scope of
an accredited institution. See Southern Association of Colleges and Schools Commission on
Colleges, 2009.

8 a.m. to 6 p.m. to allow students to receive face-to-face instruction from teaching lab assistants. In addition, instructors typically set aside regular office hours to provide students with additional opportunities to receive assistance in person. The content of the course, however, is driven by student review of materials that are available online, and much of the communication with instructors takes place by phone and email. While the program did not initially provide students with coaches, interviewees reported that they have since identified a need for stronger student supports and have thus brought on additional staff to fill this need.

Program Content and Assessment: The programs were developed to be closely aligned with the traditional course-based programs offered by TSTC, with competencies mapping directly onto traditional courses. These competencies are matched to detailed work activities as determined by employers and industry experts to ensure alignment with workforce needs. Learning objectives are then identified for each competency by faculty and industry experts. While the programs retain the learning objectives of the traditional courses, the program chairs retained faculty and administrators to develop and approve new online content. To demonstrate mastery of competencies, students engage in a variety of assessment activities across and within courses, including projects, papers, and other types of activities (e.g., hands-on demonstrations according to a checklist).

Tuition Structure: The cost of the program is $900 per semester, and students are able to take two courses per semester. Students typically pay out of pocket or through financial aid. Until recently, the program had not been approved by the Department of Education for receipt of financial aid, so the institution used grant funding to provide scholarships for students.

Austin Community College

Degree Type and Program Scope: Austin Community College offers an Accelerated Programmer Training certificate program consisting entirely of competency-based courses. Students pursuing an applied associate's degree in computer programming can also enroll in the competency-based courses, but must complete general-education coursework through the traditional courses offered at the institution. The institution chose to develop the program for two reasons: (1) a perception that they needed to develop better pathways for students who were taking too long to graduate, and that there were not a sufficient number of distance learning options; and (2) strong unmet workforce needs in the region for computer-programming expertise. In October 2012, the U.S. Department of Labor awarded a $12-million grant to a consortium with Sinclair Community College (SCC), Broward College (BC), and ACC to design competency-based IT programs based on the WGU model (Person, Goble, and Bruch, 2014).

Faculty Roles, Delivery of Instruction, and Student Supports: The majority of the courses are offered entirely online, with just one course offered through a hybrid delivery model. Courses are offered in 16-week, 12-week, and eight-week terms, though students are able to begin and end courses whenever they would like within these terms and can complete a course whenever all of the competencies are assessed as mastered. These term lengths are consistent with those for traditional courses, though students in traditional courses must begin and end courses at the same time. The program uses a learning-management system to house the curriculum and assessment materials. In addition to using the learning management system, students connect with instructors through webinar software programs, chat rooms, and by phone and email. Similar to the other programs, instructors play a guiding role, focusing efforts on students who reach out for help or otherwise indicate that they are struggling with coursework (e.g., not accessing modules, not performing well on quizzes). In addition to instructors, the institution hired two coaches to work on a regular basis with students, monitoring progress and providing supports needed to keep students on track (or referring students to other supports).

Program Content and Assessments: The courses were adapted from existing traditional programming courses, with the faculty teaching those courses leading the redesign of the coursework. According to a 2014 report, faculty are supported by an instructional designer and a multimedia specialist to develop the program content, and courses undergo a feedback and approval process to ensure the content's quality (Person, Goble, and Bruch, 2014). The institution also uses vendor-provided material. While the learning outcomes for each course and competency were largely based on existing courses, institution staff did work with industry experts to develop the competencies, and the competencies were also mapped to industry standards for certificates. The credit hours are the same for the competency-based and traditional courses. Students must complete a variety of different types of work for the courses, including assignments, lab projects, testing, group projects, and group interaction. All assessments used to assess mastery of competencies are proctored in person at a testing center.

Tuition Structure: While the program is a departure from traditional programs in design and delivery, the tuition structure remains traditional, with students paying $80 per semester credit hour, regardless of the time required to complete the course. Administrators report that the institution is looking into the possibility of transitioning to a subscription rate.

Lone Star College

Degree Type and Program Scope: Lone Star College decided to pursue competency-based education when it was invited to participate in a project with Western Governors University funded approached by the Bill & Melinda Gates Foundation. The project included 11 other colleges across the country that developed competency-based education programs, along with Lone Star and Austin, with an offer of funding to support program development. This grant also required using WGU as a model for the new programs. The institution developed programs in two areas: an IT program that leads to a certificate, and a business program that leads to an associate's degree and can articulate to a four-year bachelor degree program in business at certain universities. These specific fields were selected jointly by the group of community colleges working with the foundation.

Faculty Roles, Delivery of Instruction, and Student Supports: All of the courses in Lone Star's competency-based degree programs are provided online. Similar to ACC, courses are provided in 16-week, 14-week, 12-week, and eight-week terms to facilitate students' learning at different paces. For example, if a student has already mastered many of the competencies prior to entering the course and is therefore able to complete it in eight weeks or less, he or she has the option to enroll in a new course from one of the later terms during the same semester. Students are supported by course instructors and coaches, with instructors assigned to particular courses and coaches assigned to particular students. Similar to the other Texas programs, the instructors play a guiding role in directing students to materials, answering questions as needed, and grading assessments, while coaches provide advising and support to students on a range of academic and nonacademic issues throughout their time in the program.

Program Content and Assessments: The course content was primarily developed by faculty members, who adapted content from existing ACC courses in IT and business to create the material for the competency-based programs. The courses map exactly onto traditional courses in the respective fields. The institution has explored working with educational software vendors to develop content, but continues to rely mostly on internally developed materials. The administrators we interviewed did not reference employer involvement in identifying competencies or providing input on course content.

Tuition Structure: While students are able to move through the program at variable paces, tuition continues to be charged by the credit hour. The cost per credit hour is $80.

Student Experiences in One Texas Program

To provide a picture of student experiences with competency-based education, we interviewed nine students from one of Texas's existing competency-based programs. Students were asked about their reasons for joining the program and their experiences with the competency-based format, including self-pacing, quality and rigor, and subscription-based tuition models. The interview protocol is included in the Appendix. Below we summarize some of the key themes that emerged from student interviews.

Student Background and Entry into the Program

The students we spoke with were all nontraditional students; all were working adults ages 25 or older, and several had dependents. When we asked the students what types of individuals were most likely to be successful in competency-based programs, they universally reported that it was appropriate for students like them—working adults with family responsibilities. Interviewees responded that older students were more likely to have the self-discipline required for a self-paced program. This mirrors assertions in the literature that suggest that competency-based programs may be best suited for nontraditional students (Person, Goble, and Bruch, 2014). In addition, the ability to apply learning directly at work was viewed as important by several of the students. The majority of the students reported prior experience with college; some had left college before completing a degree or certificate, while others had completed prior degree and certificate programs. According to approximately half of our interviewees, this prior college experience was useful because the students knew what was required to complete a course. This experience helped guide them in the self-paced structure of competency-based programs. It was reported that the ability to regularly access the Internet was another important factor in determining whether the program was appropriate for a student.

Students learned of the programs in various ways. At least two of the nine students we interviewed reported hearing about the program from newspaper articles, and one reported finding the program through Facebook.

The reasons for enrolling in the program varied. Many cited career-related reasons for enrolling in the program, including wanting to enter a new career that had certain educational requirements for entry, moving up within a current organization, or performing better in a new management position. Others reported a bachelor's degree as a personal goal, something "on a bucket list," or something the student had wanted to do as an example for their teenage children. The location of the program at a respected college with traditional degree programs was cited as important to several of the students. The students referred to other online degree programs as "fly by night" and were concerned that a degree from for-profit institutions would not be taken seriously.

Some students mentioned that they were not explicitly aware of some of the competency-based aspects of the program at the time of enrollment, and in some cases were not informed about some of these aspects during their first few terms. For example, some students were unaware that they could move directly to the posttest if they had mastered a competency and of the availability of tutoring resources. Given that all of the students we spoke with were enrolled as initial cohorts when program materials were still being developed, they may have faced particular information deficits. According to our interviews with administrators, there are now more explicit efforts to provide information upfront about these aspects of the program.

Perceptions of the Benefits and Concerns Related to Competency-Based Education

The students we spoke with generally felt very positively about the program. They all said that they would recommend the program to others, and at least three of the students we spoke with had already recommended the program to coworkers. The most commonly cited benefits of the program included (1) low cost, (2) the convenience and flexibility of studying at one's own pace through an online platform, (3) the ability to move more quickly through courses than one can when required to engage in what one student referred to as "busywork," and (4) the applied focus that makes the material immediately usable in daily employment. One student also mentioned the support that was provided by staff as an attractive feature of the program.

Despite their satisfaction with the competency-based programs, interviewees also stressed that traditional programs are important to maintain. Except for one individual, all students in the sample had prior experience in traditional degree and certificate programs. One student argued that traditional-degree programs are better suited for theoretical material and allow students to gain deeper knowledge of a particular subject. Three students also mentioned a lack of interaction in competency-based degree programs, both with instructors and with students. One student described the program as "much less social." Additional face-to-face support from instructors was described as particularly important when students are struggling with material. While the interviewees all reported that they would recommend the program, most noted that the degree program was not the right fit for every student. As described in the previous section, students did not think that the program was appropriate for younger, inexperienced students because the individualized format and limited interaction with others might not provide the structured environment that some younger students may need. In addition, younger students may not have the same ability to benefit from the applied nature of the coursework if they cannot immediately apply it in a work environment.

Perceptions of Quality and Rigor

Generally, students reported that the quality and rigor of the competency-based degree program was equivalent to what they have experienced in a traditional degree program. As might be expected with any program, the students reported that the rigor varied by course and content area; some courses were reported to be less challenging and easy to move through quickly, while others were reported to require substantial time and support to master. Some of the perceived variation in rigor may be due to academic fit, as students attributed many of their challenges to a lack of experience or comfort with the material. For example, one student mentioned "not feeling comfortable with writing essays," so the courses that emphasize writing were challenging for him.

Three students mentioned mathematics as a subject in which they struggled. These students pursued tutoring as a source of additional support, but continued to struggle to complete the course. The three students who struggled in math mentioned a range of challenges, including a lack of preparation in the area, an impression that courses were disconnected, and errors in the assessment material. Based on student feedback, this institution is currently in the process of redesigning the math modules to be more coherent, with additional support materials.

Several students reported that they did not have the ability to assess the quality of the material, but thought that it was not of lower quality than they would expect from a traditional program. One student argued that the relative quality of programs depends on how you define the quality of education. If quality were defined as building applied knowledge and skills, then competency-based programs were of equal or greater quality. If quality was defined as providing deep theoretical knowledge on a particular subject, however, a traditional program might provide higher-quality education. Several students reported that they considered the applied nature of the material and its applicability to what is needed in the workplace to be an aspect of the program that enhances its quality.

Experiences with Staff Support

According to the students we spoke with, the program used the student-centered model that is common to competency-based degree programs, in which students were supported by content instructors and coaches. The instructors played more of a mentoring role, using a student's pretest results to provide initial guidance to students on available resources. As one student described it, "The instructor just gives you the tools; the student has to use them." The student-instructor contact throughout the term was typically driven by students reaching out to instructors as needed. Students reported, however, that this varied somewhat by instructor, with some preferring to more regularly touch base with students to assess progress and emerging needs. Communication typically took place by phone, email, and through the learning-management system. The student-instructor relationship also differed according to student needs and preferences. Some students suggested that regular office hours and opportunities to interact in person with instructors would be useful in offering additional support. For courses that are particularly challenging (e.g., mathematics), three of the students argued that a face-to-face or hybrid environment might be optimal to provide students with the extra in-person support that was needed.

All of the students reported that instructors provided adequate support, and they felt comfortable going to instructors with any type of question. Approximately half of the students we spoke with reported that they had little need for interaction with instructors outside of the basic guidance they provided and preferred to work independently. Four of the students mentioned that instructors provided valuable feedback on assignments that helped the student to understand expectations and perform well on later assessments. Students also mentioned, however, that their experiences with instructors varied. Some instructors were perceived to be more supportive than others, and students mentioned challenges with communication in some cases. One student reported that an instructor's lack of clarity about expectations slowed his progress early in the course. Two students described challenges with timing, arguing that lags in communication and assignment grading hindered their progress, and the lack of certainty about when an instructor would respond was frustrating. We confirmed with the institution that there are policies requiring instructors to respond to students within 24 to 48 hours of receiving an email, but administrators acknowledged that they had faced challenges with communication by certain instructors.

Coaches also play an important support role for many students. All but one of the students reported that the coaches were particularly important when students first entered the program, providing students with guidance on course selection and orienting students to the features of the competency-based approach. After the initial advising sessions, two students reported having little interaction with coaches (by preference of the student). Coaches were, however, more likely to proactively check in with students than the instructors. Other students had much more interaction with coaches, regularly working with the coach to overcome challenges and receive guidance and support on a range of issues. These students tended to be the same students who more regularly interacted with instructors. According to this group of students, the coaches were essential to their success in the program, often to a greater degree than the content instructors. Assistance with specific questions about coursework tended to be addressed by instructors or tutors, while coaches focused on program advising, course selection, and general support with personal and educational issues.

Three of the students we spoke with used tutoring services for particular courses. Students were referred to an online commercial tutoring service by the institution as a part of the program; interaction with tutors took place through a web portal. The assignment of tutors was typically random (based on availability), though there were opportunities to request a particular tutor. Experiences with tutors were mixed; one student reported that the tutor was very useful, while another student reported that the feedback from instructors was usually much more helpful than what he received from the tutors. It is unclear whether these experiences are specific to competency-based students or are representative of tutoring experiences for all students. Several students mentioned a lack of awareness about the availability of tutors, and one student suggested that the institution provide more information on the tutoring services, as he had thought the services to be a scam when contacted by the tutoring company.

Finally, seven of the students mentioned occasional interaction with administrative support staff, such as financial aid advisors, registrars, and IT support. These resources were basic services that were available to all students in the institution and were not specifically targeted to students in competency-based programs. These interactions typically occurred in response to an issue, such as a student being incorrectly billed for multiple terms or challenges with access to or content on the learning management system. According to administrators, competency-based students were particularly likely to face challenges with administrative processes due to the unique elements of these programs. Students reported that the staff were responsive to their needs, and they hypothesized that many of the administrative challenges and issues with technology were due to the newness of the program, arguing that things would likely run more smoothly for future enrollees.

Experiences with Tuition

Students universally reported that they liked the subscription-based tuition structure, and two students reported that the low cost of the program was the primary reason for choosing that institution and program. One student reported that the tuition was desirable because it fell just under the allowance provided by his employer; another student reported dropping out of another online program due to the high cost. The students who moved more quickly through the program were particularly enthusiastic about the low per-course cost that resulted from the "all you can eat" nature of a subscription model. A number of students mentioned predictability and regularity of payments as benefits of the subscription model relative to other programs where tuition varies with credit hours. As noted above, several students did experience initial challenges with financial aid (e.g., verifying enrollment status, receiving payments with a rolling calendar) and attributed these challenges to the institution's lack of experience with the program's shorter terms and subscription-based model. The students who experienced these challenges reported that they have since been resolved.

State Efforts to Facilitate Competency-Based Higher Education

States can play important roles in supporting or constraining institutions as they pursue competency-based programs. Many states have the power to encourage or discourage the development of competency-based programs through mechanisms, such as institution- and program-level approval processes and state financial-aid policies. The THECB has taken actions in several areas to support the development of competency-based programs, including establishing competency-based institutions, assisting in the development of competency-based programs, supporting the approval of competency-based programs, and participating in national discussions on competency-based education. We describe each of these efforts below.

Establishing Western Governors University in Texas

Western Governors University was originally established in 1997 in Utah. In August 2011, Governor Rick Perry founded a branch of WGU in Texas with Executive Order RP 75 to increase Texas students' participation in the institution's competency-based degree programs (Executive Order RP-75, 2011). The executive order requires the THECB to "recognize, endorse and support online, competency-based education as an important component of the state's higher-education system; to work to eliminate any unnecessary barriers to WGUs' delivery of such education programs; and to work with WGU to integrate its academic programs and services into the state's higher-education policy and strategy." According to WGU administrators, the institution has a statewide articulation agreement with all community and technical colleges. The branch of WGU in Texas has an Austin-based advisory board appointed by the governor and a Texas chancellor.

As part of the agreement to establish a state branch of WGU, the institution agreed that it will not apply for state financial aid. There have, however, been discussions of expanding financial aid to WGU, with a 2013 bill calling for a study into the feasibility of doing so (Senate Bill No. 215, 2013). The other five institutions offering competency-based degree or certificate programs in Texas are public institutions that qualify for state financial aid.

Developing the Texas A&M Commerce and South Texas College Programs

The decision for the state to get involved with directly supporting the development of competency-based degree programs was spurred by a call by Texas Governor Rick Perry for a $10,000 degree. This challenge inspired many higher education institutions in the state to rethink their current degree program offerings and their approaches to delivering education. The THECB developed a proposal for a grant from the EDUCAUSE Next Generation Learning Challenge and decided to partner with TAMUC and STC. The grant requires institutions to find new ways to improve college readiness and completion through technology-enabled approaches. In 2011, a grant was awarded to the College for All Texans Foundation to develop competency-based program through a partnership between the THECB and the two institutions.

The THECB played a significant role in many aspects of the design and implementation of the TAMUC and STC programs, including securing grant funding and fulfilling grant-reporting requirements, helping to facilitate curriculum development and leading communication with the vendors developing curriculum content, troubleshooting various implementation challenges, and acting as the point of contact for media inquiries.

The THECB played a central role in overseeing the development of the program structure and curriculum. The institutions and the THECB identified two stakeholder groups to lead the program design, one to oversee the design of the general education coursework and one to oversee the design of the upper-division coursework. The general-education working group was drawn from faculty in the various disciplines; they were asked to identify competencies by determining what a student would be expected to know upon completion of general education coursework in a particular area. The upper-division stakeholder group included faculty, employers, and representatives from K–12 school districts to ensure that the coursework was aligned with pre-college learning and employer expectations. These stakeholders were asked to identify competencies by identifying the types of jobs graduates from the program would have and determining the competencies a student would need to perform well in those jobs. The goal when developing the competencies was to emphasize application and understanding of employment contexts. The THECB's role in the development of competencies was to provide stakeholder groups and institutional administrative staff with basic informational sessions on competencies and the development of competency-based programs and to facilitate the stakeholders' meetings to identify the competencies.

Faculty worked with the education publishing company Pearson to develop the learning materials contained in the modules. The THECB facilitated the curriculum-design meetings and production development with Pearson and also conducted a review of the modules for consistency. TAMUC and STC reviewed the modules for consistency and quality and had final approval over the content.

The THECB also provided support to the institutions on a range of implementation issues. Much of this assistance was focused on navigating the issue of accreditation and whether the programs would be viewed as "substantive change." In addition, the integration of competency-based students into existing data systems and administrative processes has been a challenge that institutions continue to work to address, and the THECB has provided support and guidance on these challenges. The state was also largely responsible for the marketing and press around the programs; the programs received substantial public attention.

Approving Competency-Based Programs

The THECB is responsible for approving new degree programs in Texas based on evidence of need and likelihood of sustainability. Institutions must submit evidence in five different realms: job-market need, existing program offerings, student demand, student recruitment capacity, and enrollment projections. Associate- and certificate-level programs can engage in a streamlined process and are typically approved automatically as long as they have evidence in each of these five areas; bachelor- and master-level programs and programs with investment costs that exceed $2 million are held to stricter scrutiny and must complete a full application with more rigorous evidence requirements. In the case that competency-based programs are developed as new degree programs rather than simply new delivery mechanisms for existing programs, institutions are required to undergo the standard review process. There are no additional requirements for program approval based on a program's status as competency based. As competency-based degree programs expand in the state, the THECB will continue to evaluate the need for programs and their likelihood of sustainability, factors that are considered in the approval of traditional degree programs as well.

Institutions developing certain types of programs must also undergo the process of substantive change with the regional accreditor, SACSCOC. According to the SACSCOC website, the substantive-change process is triggered when there is a "significant modification or expansion of the nature and scope of an accredited institution" (SACSCOC, 2009). While the Texas programs were being developed, there was substantial confusion over whether the competency-based programs met the threshold for a substantive change. TAMUC and STC were in discussions with SACSCOC for nearly a year to determine whether their competency-based programs represented substantive change; there was uncertainty about whether the self-paced coursework, assessment-based progression, and alternative tuition structure qualified the programs for the process. The THECB played a central role in coordinating with institutions and accreditors to resolve the confusion.

Ultimately the institutions were not required to go through the substantive-change process, as SACSCOC has clarified that the substantive-change trigger occurs primarily when the program is a direct-assessment program. These programs represent a significant change from the typical structure of degree programs based on credit hours. By mapping competencies directly to courses and ensuring that students are awarded credit hours as they would from a traditional course, the other institutions were able to circumvent an additional review from accreditors. In the future, the THECB may need to continue to play a role in coordinating with institutions and accreditors to ensure a common understanding of the requirements for competency-based programs to undergo accreditation and to identify ways to streamline the process.

Convening with National Stakeholders

In addition to efforts to support competency-based program development within the state, the THECB and the partner institutions are part of the Competency-Based Education Network, an effort funded by the Lumina Foundation to "provide an evidence-based approach to advancing high-quality competency-based education capable of serving many more students of all backgrounds." The group was formed in 2013, and they convene on a periodic basis to share lessons learned, work together to address common implementation challenges, and develop practitioner-based research. THECB staff have used these discussions to inform decisionmaking about state policy efforts around competency-based education and disseminate information to institutions.

Summary

In this chapter, we summarized the recent expansion efforts around competency-based education in Texas. We first described the competency-based programs at the six institutions offering these programs in Texas. The programs were similar across many characteristics, such as self-paced progression, personalized learning approaches, and reliance on a range of assessments to determine mastery of competencies. On the other hand, the programs also differ on characteristics, such as method of course delivery, faculty roles, and tuition structures. We also described the role the THECB has played in allowing for (and in some cases supporting) the development of competency-based programs, with activities that included negotiation with accreditors, approval of programs, and establishment of a new competency-based institution.

In addition to describing the experiences of institutions and the THECB staff in implementing the competency-based programs, we described student experiences from a small sample of students in one competency-based degree program. In general, we found that students reported positive experiences with the program and would recommend the program to others. Students liked the convenience and flexibility of the program, the ability to move through a low-cost program at one's own pace, and the applied nature of the content. Students reported that the program was rigorous, perceived it as being of similar quality to traditional programs, and most were satisfied with the support that was provided by coaches. Students also reported challenges, including varied experiences with instructors and tutors, administrative processes, and coursework. In addition, some students missed the more social nature of traditional programs, and many students reported that competency-based programs may not be appropriate for students who lack the maturity and experiences that enable students to work through self-paced, student-centered programs.

In the next chapter, Chapter Four, we pull together findings from the literature, administrator and student interviews, and program documentation to identify key challenges to the implementation and success of competency-based programs. We also suggest policy and research efforts that may be useful in supporting the effective and efficient expansion of competency-based education programs in Texas and in other states that may consider moving in this direction.

CHAPTER FOUR

A Path Forward for Competency-Based Education in Texas

The previous chapters provided information on the current landscape for competency-based higher-education programs in Texas, including descriptions of existing programs, a summary of state efforts to support these programs, and student experiences in one of these programs. By placing the experiences of Texas programs in the context of prior literature, we now identify key challenges common to competency-based programs, as well as some lessons learned on minimizing those challenges. We also identify several policy efforts that may be useful in supporting competency-based education programs and provide suggestions for research to determine whether these programs are effective at meeting employer and student needs and are sustainable.

Programs Face a Common Set of Challenges

According to interviews with administrators, a staff member of the THECB, and students, institutions faced a variety of challenges as they developed competency-based degree and certificate programs. The challenges described by Texas stakeholders are similar to those described in the literature as challenges for other institutions with competency-based programs. From our interviews and the literature we identified the most commonly mentioned challenges; we group these challenges into in seven categories, described below.

A Need to Alter Administrative Systems and Processes

The most commonly cited challenge with the implementation of competency-based programs in Texas was the adoption of new administrative software and processes to accommodate the unique needs of students in such programs. The move away from credit hours, varying course lengths, and different grading mechanisms are some the characteristics of competency-based programs that are particularly challenging to harmonize with existing administrative systems. Administrators and students reported that they faced significant challenges with registering students, processing financial aid, and collecting data on student progress. The ability to support competency-based students in administrative systems has been limited by a lack of software that can accommodate these students and difficulty implementing flexible processes and procedures that can meet the needs of students in traditional and competency-based programs. Institutions in Texas have worked to overcome inertia among support staff who are accustomed to executing administrative processes that rely on standard term lengths and student course loads. The need to overhaul administrative systems and the need to retrain support staff were also the most commonly cited challenges in the literature (Bergeron, 2013; Council for Adult and Experiential Learning, 2014; Johnstone and Soares, 2014; Klein-Collins, 2013; Person, Goble, and Bruch, 2014).

Challenges with Federal, Regional, and State Oversight

Institutions in Texas also faced challenges with oversight from the U.S. Department of Education, regional accreditors, and the THECB. With regard to federal oversight, TSTC faced substantial challenges with delays in approval for federal financial aid. TSTC is not alone; financial-aid approval has been a challenge for many direct-assessment programs because the financial-aid system was built around the credit hour (Klein-Collins, 2013). According to administrators, the institution used grant funds in the first year of the program to provide scholarships to students who were interested in enrolling but could not obtain financial aid. For programs that choose not to tie their competencies to credit hours, the literature describes several other approaches to obtaining approval for financial aid (Klein-Collins, 2013, and

Laitinen, 2012). Institutions can work with the Department of Education to apply for the direct-assessment provision.[1] According to Klein-Collins (2013), the first college to successfully have an application approved under this provision was Southern New Hampshire University, which was approved in April 2013. Other approaches include the Department of Education designating institutions as "experimental" and allowing them to test financial aid options for direct-assessment programs and working with the Department of Education to redefine the credit hour.[2]

A second challenge to several of the institutions, and many institutions across the country, has been regional accreditation. The program at TSTC had to be approved because it was a direct-assessment program, and the need for approval by the TAMUC and STC programs was unclear, leading to delays in program launch. Since WGU was originally "located" in two different states and had 19 states affiliated with it, the institution was required to have four different regional accrediting associations review it. It is now accredited by only the Northwest Association of Schools and Colleges. Some regional accreditors have been hesitant to approve direct-assessment programs and report that they are receiving mixed messages from the federal government on the criteria for direct assessment approval (Klein-Collins, 2013). Competency-based programs represent a substantial departure from the traditional accreditation process, which largely focuses on course materials, faculty qualifications, and other input-related characteristics. Institutions in Texas, however, have been able to avoid the substantive-change process by mapping competencies to courses and credit hours and ensuring that faculty retain a somewhat traditional

---

[1] For a description of the application process, see U.S. Department of Education, 2013.

[2] Congress authorized the Experimental Sites Initiative under section 487A(b) of the Higher Education Act of 1965. This initiative tests the effectiveness of statutory and regulatory flexibility for participating institutions disbursing Title IV student aid. The Department of Education waives specific statutory or regulatory requirements at the postsecondary institutions, or consortia of institutions, approved to participate in the experiments. A Federal Register notice released in July 2014 invites institutions with competency-based programs and limited direct assessment programs to apply for experimental status (see U.S. Department of Education, July 2014).

role in course development. A clear, consistent accreditation policy for different types of competency-based education programs is needed to ensure that institutions are able to clearly understand accreditation procedures. According to the Texas stakeholders we talked with, many of the initial challenges with accreditation have begun to be resolved as more institutions have moved through the process of developing competency-based programs.

For the most part, administrators at institutions described the THECB as a facilitator of their efforts to develop competency-based degree programs. The THECB does, however, require institutions to report student-level data on a variety of different aspects of student progress, and program leadership noted that it was initially a challenge to determine how to integrate reporting for competency-based students. The THECB has worked with institutions to develop modifications to their reporting requirements to accommodate the unique aspects of competency-based programs.

Adjustment to the Transformation of Faculty Roles

Given the student-centered and personalized nature of many competency-based programs, faculty roles place additional emphasis on mentoring. Building support among faculty for competency-based programs can be a challenge, but an essential one to overcome as many of the institutions argued that it is critical for faculty to play a central role in planning and designing competency-based programs. According to the administrators we interviewed and the literature, faculty members are often familiar with a particular approach to teaching and can be skeptical that student-centered approaches can achieve the same levels of success. In addition, competency-based programs can be viewed as a threat to faculty positions. It is unclear, however, whether introducing more competency-based programs truly threatens faculty jobs, as the courses may require the same level of faculty involvement while reallocating time from lecturing to student monitoring and individualized guidance.

Even when instructors are supportive of a competency-based approach, they may not have the skills required to successfully transition into new roles. Faculty can no longer expect all students to be following a common pathway through the curriculum and must adjust to personalized learning at variable paces. They are expected to now design and compile new types of content (e.g., web-based content); closely monitor student progress; and act as instructional guides, motivators, and assessment specialists. Yet many have never had experience in these areas. Some institutions, such as WGU, have a specialty-based faculty arrangement in which faculty are hired to perform one particular role (e.g., content design, assessment, student academic support). To ensure that faculty are prepared to transition to these new roles, training and support are likely important. For example, WGU provides new faculty with nearly 50 hours of training in the first few weeks after they are hired; then they work side by side with an experienced faculty member for several months before they work with their own students. Institutions may also need to carefully consider how they go about staffing their competency-based programs. Institutions can determine not only what roles instructors will play, but also whether they should be full-time or part-time (i.e., teaching traditional courses alongside work in competency-based programs).

The Need to Create and Manage Program Content and Assessments

Some argue that continuous access to program content is a critical feature of self-paced instruction (Johnstone and Soares, 2014). Most of the institutions in Texas have moved to fully online delivery to facilitate content access and self-paced learning. The move to online learning and the shift to competency-driven content typically require new course material and assessments that are tied to each competency. As noted above, instructors typically play an important role in developing the course content. In some cases, internal staff are primarily responsible for the design and/or collection of course materials (e.g., ACC, WGU), while in other cases the instructors help to guide and review the work of vendors. To support faculty in their new roles as content designers, many of the institutions have developed handbooks and trainings or hired media experts. Institutions must purchase or develop learning-management systems to provide continuous online access to course content and facilitate communication and tracking of student progress, and in some cases we heard from institutions that these learning-management systems presented some technical challenges when first launching the program.

While none of the Texas stakeholders mentioned assessment design and security as a challenge, this was emphasized in the literature as a challenge for the competency-based education sector (Johnstone and Soares, 2014, and Porter and Reilly, 2014). The effectiveness of competency-based programs and their graduates depends largely on the ability of assessments to successfully measure mastery of a competency. In addition to ensuring the quality and rigor of the assessments, institutions must develop processes to secure the assessments and proctor exams. Several of the Texas institutions require in-person proctoring to ensure assessments are secure.

The Need for Enhanced Student Support

Because competency-based programs are typically self-paced, administrators argued that they require a level of student support beyond what is provided for traditional programs. While only two of the students we spoke with emphasized the role of the instructor as being essential to their success, all but one reported that the role of the coach was critically important. Support was reported to be particularly important in the early stages of enrollment as students oriented themselves with competency-based education. In addition, coaches are often in more regular, proactive contact with students throughout the program than are content instructors and play roles as advisors, mentors, motivators, and monitors. One institution reported that one of their early missteps was to not hire coaches; the program soon realized the need for additional student support and hired the necessary staff. The institutions view coaching as a critical resource, and as programs increase in size, the support may need to be scaled. Yet many institutions already face substantial challenges with providing the advising that is needed for traditional programs given high advisor-to-student ratios on many college campuses. Finding sustainable ways to continue providing student support is a challenge that institutions are likely to continue to face. In addition, career counseling must look somewhat different for competency-based programs according to several of the stakeholders we interviewed, given that these students are typically nontraditional mid-career students who are looking to advance or transition to a new career.

Requirements for Stronger Connections with Employers

Though less often emphasized as a challenge, interviewees reported that they did need to build new relationships with employers to ensure an industry-relevant, competency-based degree program. The literature on competency-based programs suggests that employers have typically played a role in the process of identifying competencies, particularly for the field-specific content. If the competencies are not aligned with employer needs, then competency-based programs may be no better at meeting workforce needs than traditional programs. In addition to playing a central role in program development, employers can refer enrollees for competency-based programs. These programs are often intended for mid-career individuals who are moving up within companies or need training. Employers can benefit from partnering with institutions to build the skill base of their workforce, while institutions can benefit from the additional enrollment that these employer relationships might provide.

Challenges with Enrollment and Sustainability

Several stakeholders reported that marketing competency-based programs was a challenge. Administrators reported that the unique attributes of competency-based programs can be difficult to explain. In addition, if the assumption that these programs are best suited for nontraditional students is true, this population may be more diffuse and challenging to reach. Administrators attributed low levels of enrollment in several of the programs to marketing challenges. Several of the students mentioned having first heard of the program in newspaper articles, and the students reported bringing in new enrollees through word of mouth. Several institutions mentioned that partnerships with and marketing to employers was a potentially successful approach that they were planning to use to increase enrollment.

More generally, the literature describes the sustainability of competency-based programs as a significant challenge (HCM Strategists, 2013, and Porter and Reilly, 2014). According to Porter and

Reilly (2014), sustainability depends on a number of different aspects. These programs have substantial upfront costs to build the systems and content, train staff, and market. In addition, institutions in Texas typically hired additional support staff to coach students. It is unclear whether programs can be scaled to the level that will be necessary to recoup these costs. Online learning can provide economies of scale by delivering content to a large number of students for a small additional cost per student. The ability of students to move through coursework quickly, however, sometimes on an "all you can eat" basis, may mean lower per-student revenues. Book (2014) argues that institutions must be careful to design tuition structures that ensure sustainability.

Experiences of Existing Programs Offer Lessons

Our interviews with institutional administrators and THECB staff as well as prior literature on competency-based education suggest that there are a number of lessons that can be learned from the experiences of existing programs. Drawing on our notes and the literature, we summarize five lessons.

Build Understanding and Buy-In Among Institutional Stakeholders

As noted in the previous section, one of the major challenges reported by institutions is the institutional culture that is accustomed to a traditional academic structure (e.g., credit hours, lecture-based instruction). Texas stakeholders and the literature argue that faculty and support staff must play a central role in the design and implementation of competency-based programs. To ensure that they embrace the program and make the transitions necessary to provide high-quality competency-based education, one institution stressed that it was important to bring staff on very early in the process, and it can be useful to identify a core set of individuals who could advocate for and take ownership of the program. To ensure that institutional staff had the information they needed, many institutions have developed orientation sessions, trainings, and guides to systematically provide information to stakeholders.

According to the literature, there are a number of factors that can influence buy-in among faculty and support staff and shift institutional culture. For the most part, the literature on building support for competency-based programs in higher education mirrors the general literature on organizational change. For example, one lesson learned from a study of ten higher-education programs is the importance of strong leadership support (Book, 2014). Porter and Reilly (2014) also found that successful programs typically had support from external stakeholders, and they recommend that programs draw support from external governing bodies and employers. To ensure that institutional staff understand the reasoning for the program and are supportive of its development, it is important to demonstrate how the competency-based programs are aligned with the mission of the institution, and a strong argument must be made for why the program will enhance the institution while remaining cohesive with other institutional efforts (Book, 2014).

Leverage Key Resources to Develop Content

The substantial resources required to develop competency-based programs are largely driven by the need to identify the key competencies and develop the program content. One Texas interviewee noted that it is critical to identify all of the competencies that will result from a program early on, rather than trying to piecemeal programs together course by course. Institutions can then leverage a range of different resources to facilitate the efficient development of course content. According to several institutions, employers played a role in the identification of competencies. For some fields, institutions can also turn to industry standards and certification exams to structure their competency-based programs. Texas institutions have also referenced existing courses to define learning outcomes and identify course material. Wooten and Elden (2003) argue that the use of previously developed models and taxonomies can lead to substantial savings in terms of costs to develop the content for programs.

Carefully Select and Inform Students

With the exception of the TSTC, competency-based degree programs have primarily enrolled adult students, many who are employed and have their own family. According to students and administrators, adult students with prior education and workforce experience can leverage existing knowledge, skills, and abilities to move more quickly through the programs, and these students often have the ability to directly apply what they are learning in their current place of employment. In addition, administrators, students, and the literature argued that adult students have the maturity and self-control required to remain motivated and focused in self-paced, student-driven environments. Nontraditional students are also more likely to benefit from the flexibility of self-paced, online programs because they may have jobs, families, and other responsibilities that are likely to prevent them from enrolling in traditional programs. Experts and stakeholders involved with competency-based education agree that particular types of students, including older students and those with prior educational or work experience, have the greatest potential to benefit from these types of programs (Person, Goble, and Bruch, 2014). As institutions consider marketing and enrollment requirements, it may be useful to focus these efforts on the students who are most likely to be successful.

In addition to recruiting and enrolling individuals who have certain characteristics, it is important to ensure that students have a clear understanding of how the program works and how to leverage the benefits of the alternative model. The student interviews revealed that several students were not aware of the competency-based aspects of the program, and they had primarily enrolled because it was an online program from a reputable institution. Some were unaware that they could move directly to posttest if they had mastered a competency, that tutoring was available, and even that they were in a competency-based program. Some Texas institutions have begun to offer student orientations, a practice mentioned in the literature as useful (Johnstone and Soares, 2014). Coaches also appear to have played an important role in informing students about the unique aspects of their competency-based programs.

Enhance Student Tracking and Support Systems

Many of the stakeholders we interviewed as well as the literature suggest that student support may be particularly important in competency-based programs where students have substantial autonomy. These programs may require institutions to hire additional support staff beyond what is typically available in traditional programs, and coaches and instructors likely need training to use the data available to provide real-time assistance to students as necessary. According to the evidence we collected, it is important to have support staff involved early in the design and implementation of the program to ensure buy-in and informed development of the support process and to consider the necessary data systems in these initial stages as well. Book (2014) notes that while faculty are typically involved early in the process of developing competency-based programs, support staff are often not brought in until the program begins to enroll students.

According to Texas stakeholders and the literature, the adaptation of data systems is essential to providing strong student support within competency-based programs (Book, 2014). It is critical for institutional staff to regularly track the progress of their students and identify when help is needed. In addition, data systems can help to identify the characteristics associated with student success and target services accordingly. Yet as described previously, institutions faced considerable challenges with developing student-administrative systems and student-tracking systems that could accommodate the unique aspects of competency-based programs. Institutions should work early in the development of the program to develop these data systems to effect student support.

Continuously Assess the Program

As Johnson and Soares (2014) highlight, there is a need to continuously assess the programs and make improvements as necessary. One Texas institution reported that they have check-in meetings between terms and on a monthly basis as an opportunity to debrief and make changes. Another institution recommends launching programs slowly and starting with a single field to ensure the ability to track metrics and determine what is working and what is not. Where competency-based education programs are found to be successful, this evidence can be used to build support for new programs or to potentially adopt some aspects of competency-based education in the traditional programs. Finally, because competency-based degree programs are often designed to be closely aligned with employer needs, it will be critical to stay informed about industry changes.

A Way Forward for Competency-Based Education in Texas

Competency-based programs across Texas and the rest of the United States have developed a range of innovative approaches to higher education that may help to provide new, potentially effective pathways to degrees and certificates while also controlling or reducing the cost for students. A shift to competencies can ensure that institutions are outcomes focused and are offering programs aligned with the needs of employers. The assessment of students on a well-defined set of competencies may help to ensure that graduates have the knowledge, skills, and abilities desired in the workforce. Student-centered learning and self-paced coursework provide individuals with an environment that facilitates personalized learning. And innovative approaches to tuition have the potential to improve program accessibility for resource-constrained students. These programs provide an alternative pathway for many students who might not otherwise succeed in higher education.

Yet competency-based programs can be challenging to develop, as the programs must adopt new administrative systems and processes, reimagine faculty roles, and provide additional student support. Many U.S. higher-education policies center on the credit hour, and institutions that move away from the credit hour face challenges with financial aid, accreditation, and articulation. Direct-assessment programs face an additional layer of challenges because these programs seek to completely separate their programs from the credit hour. As the government, accreditors, and institutions become more familiar with competency-based education, some of these barriers to direct-assessment programs may subside.

While competency-based education in Texas is growing, it is not likely to overtake traditional approaches to education. With the exception of WGU, none of the Texas institutions we studied is likely to move to whole-institution reform. These programs provide a new pathway that has primarily demonstrated success with older working adults, and many stakeholders argued that it may not be the best approach for younger students who are first entering college. In addition, some expressed opinions that competency-based degree and certificate programs may be more appropriate for certain fields, such as those that are more applied, and some of the most challenging higher-education material may benefit from additional in-person support. According to the literature, there are concerns about sustainability as well, suggesting that institutions are not likely to replace traditional programs.

Addressing Policies

As with any new educational arena, the evolution of competency-based education, whether it be direct assessment or course based, raises a number of challenges to current higher-education administrative systems and policies, be it at the institutional, state, or federal level.

Institutional Policies

As described above, institutions implementing competency-based education have encountered substantial challenges with data systems, administrative procedures, and the development of curriculum, as existing tools and institutional policies are not able to easily accommodate some features of competency-based education. Institutions may need to examine attendance policies, financial aid procedures, and business processes and practices. For those institutions that move toward a subscription-based tuition and fee model, the need to study the impact on business processes and practices will be crucial. Billing and payment cycles may have to be rearranged for students in a competency-based program. Institutions using nonstandard term lengths for competency programs will need to examine the impact of those terms on their financial aid and business processes as well as the impact on the admissions calendar. Processes for administration and curriculum development must be adapted to ensure that the needs of competency-based programs and their enrollees can be met.

Institutions may also need to address academic and admission policies. For example, transfer policies vary greatly from institution to institution, though all institutions have at least some limit on the number of credits that students can transfer in.[3] Institutions should determine whether the structure of their competency-based programs leads to any additional complications with credit transfer, and make efforts to address barriers. Other academic policies that might need to be examined include residency policies, incomplete policies, and policies that place a limit on the number of credit hours a student can earn during a semester.

In addition, given that competency-based programs largely target adult learners, policies for students who are being admitted to competency-based programs should reduce the barriers of enrollment that may arise for this population. For example, some institutions may set limitations on the ability to transfer credits that were earned long ago, and these restrictions may prevent returning adult students from receiving credit for prior learning regardless of whether they are able to demonstrate mastery of the material. Some returning adults may have difficulty obtaining high school transcripts, have SAT or ACT scores that are out of date, or may be unable to produce other documents typically associated with college applications and admissions. Although some of these policy interventions focus more on the needs of returning adult students rather than competency-based education specifically, a comprehensive audit of institutional practices and policies may be warranted.

State Policies

Just as institutions should benefit from a comprehensive audit of practices and policies, states interested in facilitating the growth of competency-based education could engage in a similar audit of state

---

[3] In the case of Texas public institutions, SACSCOC requires that the last 30 semester credit hours of a baccalaureate degree program be provided by the institution awarding the degree.

policies and practices. States may need to consider institutional funding, student financial aid, and statewide academic policies, such as general-education core curricula and transfer policies. For example, states with general-education core curricula requirements centered around courses and semester credit hours may need to evaluate how a non-semester credit-hour direct-assessment program would be mapped back to the core curriculum requirements. This could involve the mapping of competencies back to courses or could involve the creation of competency equivalencies for each course and the development of a competency-based core curriculum rather than a course-based curriculum. Other statewide academic policies, such as transfer compacts, may also need to be modified to create a transfer pathway for both students wishing to transfer into competency-based programs and those wishing to transfer out of these programs. Additionally, states could consider the impact of academic policies, such as limitations on semester credit hours in a term and restrictions on the retaking of courses.

Financial-aid and funding policies could also be examined. For example, states that offer direct financial aid to students, whether through loans or grants, may need to examine semester credit-hour requirements associated with those programs. For direct-assessment programs, states must address issues of how to fund students without credit-hour equivalencies. Programs with nonstandard term lengths may present challenges in terms of aid-disbursement schedules. In addition to student financial-aid policies, states may need to consider reworking the way they fund institutions, as many states fund based on credit hours and seat time. For example, many competency-based programs offer substantially shorter terms relative to traditional semester-length programs, and in order to complete coursework in these accelerated terms, students are advised to enroll in fewer courses per term. If the shorter-term length is not accounted for, and states base funding on a single-snapshot date, competency-based education students may mistakenly be counted as part-time, and institutions may not receive sufficient funding for these students. Direct-assessment programs may face additional challenges in states that fund based on semester credit hours, as these programs may be ineligible for state funding.

Federal Policies

Institutions offering competency-based education programs may also encounter challenges with federal policies, especially around financial-aid eligibility and, for online programs, state authorization. As discussed previously, the Department of Education provides an option for institutions offering direct-assessment programs to apply for financial-aid eligibility. Very few institutions, however, have been able to successfully navigate this process since it was announced in March 2013, and much confusion has existed both at the department and among institutions.[4] Institutions have questions of how aid disbursement will work with competency-based education students (e.g., when aid should be disbursed, what satisfactory academic progress should look like). In an effort to answer these questions, the Department of Education issued a call for experimental sites in July 2013. Experimental-site status will provide flexibility for institutions to develop different federal financial-aid disbursement and eligibility practices that better align with competency-based programs, especially programs that are either offered in nonstandard term lengths or use a direct-assessment model.

Federal regulations on offering online education to out-of-state students may also complicate program delivery. These policies require institutions to gain the approval of any state in which their online students reside, regardless of whether or not the institution has a physical presence in that state. Until recently this has meant that institutions had to navigate a number of very different and often-expensive state policies and authorization processes. The recent development of the National Council for State Authorization Reciprocity Agreement is attempting to streamline this process. Its success, however, is dependent upon the willingness of each state to opt in to the coalition on behalf of its higher-education institutions; as of May 2015, only 24 states had joined the council. Texas is currently not a member of the council, and legislation authorizing the THECB to join on behalf of Texas institutions must be passed in order for the state to participate.

---

[4] The Department of Education is attempting to address this confusion and issued a letter with further instructions on competency-based education and federal financial aid on December 19, 2014. See U.S. Department of Education, 2014.

Areas for Future Research

While competency-based education shows promise to deliver lower-cost higher education and add additional pathways to student completion, there is currently little research that institutions and policymakers can draw on to guide program development and implementation. The research base, including this report, consists of case studies that attempt to distill lessons learned from a handful of institutions that have implemented competency-based programs. And while these studies provide useful information about the implementation process within institutions and point to policy barriers, more research is needed to understand whether competency-based programs are effective in meeting the needs of students and employers, how they can be improved to maximize effectiveness, and whether they are cost effective and sustainable. Below we outline a broad research agenda that can inform whether and how to expand competency-based education programs and for whom.

Improving the Design and Implementation of Competency-Based Programs

Given the recent efforts to expand competency-based programs in higher education, research is needed to help institutions develop effective competency-based programs and improve the implementation of these programs. For example, institutions need to understand:

- *Student supports*: Whether and how data and analytics can be used to develop and improve student support structures and what other supports can help students to be successful in competency-based programs
- *Staffing of programs*: Whether the disaggregated faculty model that some competency-based programs employ is appropriate and how to optimize faculty and support roles to promote student success and reduce or maintain costs to institutions
- *Assessment design*: How assessments can most effectively determine whether students have gained key competencies
- *Quality assurance*: What institutional, regional, or state policies and practices may be required to monitor the quality of competency-based degree programs

- *Appropriateness of programs by field*: Whether certain fields are more suited to the development of competency-based degree programs than others
- *Improving efficiency and effectiveness*: How competency-based degree pathways can be designed to ensure that they are effective and efficient in improving completion rates.

Rigorously Assessing the Impact of Competency-Based Programs on Student Outcomes

While some studies have included student interviews and/or focus groups to understand student experiences with competency-based programs and their suggestions for improvement, there is currently no information about the outcomes of students who enter those programs. To guide further program and policy development, a series of rigorous evaluations are needed to understand the causal impact of different approaches to competency-based education programs on student outcomes, such as student learning, degree completion, and employment outcomes. In addition, there may be differential impacts for students with different characteristics (e.g., adult learners versus traditional college-aged students); researchers should identify the characteristics associated with success in competency-based programs to improve the targeting of competency-based education to those who may be able to benefit most. In addition to examining impacts on student outcomes, researchers should assess student satisfaction with competency-based programs and employer satisfaction with graduates of those programs.

Ensuring the Efficiency and Sustainability of Competency-Based Programs

Finally, research is needed to help institutions develop competency-based programs that can limit increases in college costs to students and institutions while simultaneously ensuring that these programs are sustainable. Institutions considering competency-based programs need a clearer picture of the true start-up costs associated with these programs and must be equipped with the tools to accurately project enrollments and revenue. In addition, the literature does not provide clear evidence on the relative differences in ongoing faculty and support costs associated with competency-based programs, so more research comparing the relative costs of competency-based programs and traditional programs is needed. In determining which institutions can most effectively implement competency-based programs, research is needed on the aspects of institutions (such as institutional leadership, faculty involvement, etc.) that might make them better candidates for implementing successful and sustainable competency-based degree programs. Alternatively, there are concerns that competency-based programs will threaten the sustainability of traditional programs. As competency-based programs expand in number, research can help to determine when programs are serving unmet needs and when programs are cannibalizing other programs, whether competency based or traditional.

Summary

This report documents the landscape for competency-based education in Texas, and the experiences of Texas institutions largely mirror the national literature on competency-based education programs. The institutions faced challenges in implementing these programs that ranged from inflexible administrative data systems and processes to oversight. The experiences of Texas institutions and the institutions profiled in the literature suggest several recommendations for implementing competency-based programs: (1) build understanding and buy-in among institutional stakeholders, (2) leverage key resources to develop content, (3) carefully select and inform students, (4) enhance student tracking and support systems, and (5) continuously assess the program. The research described in this report, however, is not sufficient to address all questions about competency-based programs. Additional research is needed on the effectiveness of these programs in meeting the needs of students and employers and the cost of these programs to students, institutions, and states. Institutional, state, and federal policy changes may also be warranted to support future development of competency-based programs.

Interview Protocols

Administrator Protocol

1. How did your institution decide to get into competency-based education?
2. What degree programs do you offer via competency-based education? How did you decide on those specific degree programs?
3. How is course content delivered (e.g., online, hybrid, face to face)?
4. How do students interact with instructors, coaches, and/or tutors?
5. How do students demonstrate competencies in these programs?
6. How do students pay for the program?
7. What is the demographic make up? What proportion are adult learners? Military?
8. What distinguishes your competency-based education students from traditional college students?
9. Do your competency-based education students have any unique needs or face unique challenges, and if so, what are they?
10. Are there students who you think will benefit more or less from competency-based education programs, and if so, whom?
11. Do you map competencies back to traditional degree programs and courses?

12. How does your institution develop instructional content for these programs? Do you engage faculty/instructors, course designers, packaged content?
13. How do your programs leverage technology?
14. What issues have you faced in developing competency-based education degree programs?
15. What challenges have you faced in implementing your competency-based education programs (e.g., faculty, accreditation, students, administration, support staff, financial aid, content development)?
16. How did you deal with these challenges?
17. Would you approach these challenges differently if you encountered them in the future?
18. Are there any regulatory or policy changes that you believe could improve the environment for implementation?
19. What advice would you give to other institutions that are considering developing competency-based education programs?

Student Interview Protocol

1. To start, can you tell me about your prior experiences with college?
2. Have you attended college previously?
3. What has motivated you to come to college right now?
4. Can you tell me about what work experience, if any, you have had?
5. Why did you choose a competency based degree program instead of the traditional baccalaureate degree program?
6. What are your goals and expectation of this program?
7. How does the program fit into your life?
8. Are there things that you think are better about competency based programs compared to traditional degree programs? If so, can you tell me about these things?

9. Are there things that you think are better about traditional degree programs compared to competency based programs? If so, can you tell me about these things?

10. Are there things you like about using a self-paced delivery model?

11. Have you faced any challenges using a self-paced delivery model?

12. Have you ever had difficulty in motivating yourself to complete a module or course? Why or why not?

13. Are there aspects of the program that are helpful in addressing challenges with motivation?

14. Are there things you think could be changed about the program to help address challenges with motivation?

15. Have you had challenges in completing a term?
Why or why not?

16. Any other challenges?

17. Did you find it was easy to navigate IT?

18. If you faced challenges, how did you deal with them?

19. Do you think the level of rigor in your program is easy or difficult? Why?

20. Overall, what has been your experience in the level of rigor in competency-based education courses versus traditional courses?

21. Are there particular subject or course work areas that are better suited for traditional courses because they are difficult to master through competency-based programs?

22. Based on your current and previous college experiences, do you believe the competency-based degree program has the same level of quality as a traditional degree program, a higher level of quality, or a lower level of quality?

23. Can you tell us about your relationship with your content instructors?

24. Do you feel that the instructors provide adequate support?

25. Do you feel comfortable contacting your instructor with any issues you have?

26. Do you feel that the instructor plays an important role in your learning?

27. Tell us about your experience with coaches. Do you feel that the coaches are important to your success in this program? How has your coach helped you during your time in this program?
28. Have you used a tutor during your time in this program? How helpful was this experience?
29. How has flat-rate tuition worked for you in comparison to a traditional program where you pay by the credit hour?
30. What are the benefits of the flat-rate tuition?
31. Are there any challenges with flat-rate tuition?
32. Would you recommend competency-based programs to others?
33. What type of student would you recommend enroll in a competency-based education degree program? Why so?
34. Do you have any additional thoughts to add on your experience in this program?

Abbreviations

ACC	Austin Community College
IT	information technology
SACSCOC	Southern Association of Colleges and Schools Commission on Colleges
STC	South Texas College
TAMUC	Texas A&M Commerce
THECB	Texas Higher Education Coordinating Board
TSTC	Texas State Technical College
WGU	Western Governors University

References

Baum, Sandy, and Jennifer Ma, *Trends in College Pricing, 2014*, New York: College Board, 2014.

Belfield, Clive, Vivian Yuen Ting Liu, and Madeline Joy Trimble, *The Medium-Term Labor Market Returns to Community College Awards: Evidence from North Carolina*, working paper, New York: Center for Analysis of Postsecondary Education and Employment (CAPSEE), Columbia University, March 2014.

Bell, Allison C., *What Is Competency-Based Education?* Washington, D.C.: HCM Strategists, September 2013.

Bell, Allison C., and Kristin Conklin, *State Financial Aid Programs and Competency-Based Education,* Washington, D.C.: HCM Strategists, October 2013.

Bergeron, David A., *A Path Forward: Game-Changing Reforms in Higher Education and the Implications for Business and Financing Models*, Washington, D.C.: Center for American Progress, December 2013.

Book, Patricia A., *All Hands on Deck: Ten Lessons from Early Adopters of Competency-Based Education*, Boulder, Colo.: WICHE Cooperative for Educational Technologies (WCET), May 2014.

Carnevale, Anthony P., Ban Cheah, and Andrew R. Hanson, *The Economic Value of College Majors*, executive summary, Washington, D.C.: Georgetown University, Center on Education and the Workforce, 2015.

College Board, *Trends in Student Aid, 2014*, Washington, D.C.: College Board, 2014.

Complete College America, *Time Is the Enemy*, Washington, D.C.: Complete College America, September 2011.

Council for Adult and Experiential Learning (CAEL), *Customized, Outcome-Based, Relevant Evaluation (CORE) at Lipscomb University*, Chicago, 2014.

Deming, David J., Claudia Goldin, and Lawrence F. Katz, *The For-Profit Postsecondary School Sector: Nimble Critters or Agile Predators?* Cambridge, Mass.: National Bureau of Education Research (NBER), Working Paper No. 17710, December 2011.

Executive Order RP-75, *Relating to the Establishment and Support of Western Governors University Texas*, Austin, Tex.: Governor of the State of Texas, August 3, 2011.

Fain, Paul, "Taking the Direct Path," *Inside Higher Ed*, February 21, 2014. As of December 10, 2014:
https://www.insidehighered.com/news/2014/02/21/direct-assessment-and-feds-take-competency-based-education

Hart Research Associates, *Raising the Bar: Employers' Views on College Learning in the Wake of the Economic Downturn, A Survey Among Employers Conducted on Behalf of the Association of American Colleges and Universities*, Washington, D.C.: Hart Research Associates, January 2010.

HCM Strategists, *Creating a System-Wide, Competency-Based Online Program*, Washington, D.C.: HCM Strategists, September 2013.

Johnstone, Sally M., and Louis Soares, "Principles for Developing Competency-Based Education Programs," *Change: The Magazine of Higher Learning,* Vol. 46, No. 2, April 2014, pp. 12–19.

Klein-Collins, Rebecca, *Competency-Based Degree Programs in the U.S.: Postsecondary Credentials for Measurable Student Learning and Performance*, Chicago: Council for Adult and Experiential Learning (CAEL), 2012.

———, *Sharpening Our Focus on Learning: The Rise of Competency-Based Approaches to Degree Completion*, National Institute for Learning Outcomes Assessment (NILOA), University of Illinois at Urbana-Champaign, November 2013.

Klein-Collins, Rebecca, and Elizabeth Baylor, *Meeting Students Where They Are: Profiles of Students in Competency-Based Degree Programs*, Washington, D.C.: Center for American Progress, November 2013.

Krupnick, Matt, "You Can Now Get College Credit Without Ever Taking a Class," *Time.com*, February 24, 2015. As of August 12, 2015:
http://time.com/3712544/competency-education-college-degree-programs

Laitinen, Amy, *Cracking the Credit Hour*, Washington, D.C.: New America Foundation and Education Sector, September 2012.

Long, Bridget Terry, *Addressing the Academic Barriers to Higher Education*, Washington, D.C.: The Hamilton Project, the Brookings Institution, 2014.

Lumina Foundation, *Strategic Plan, 2013–2016,* Indianapolis, Ind., 2013. As of August 18, 2015:
http://www.luminafoundation.org/files/file/2013-lumina-strategic-plan.pdf

Mitchell, Robin, and Jill Sinclair Bell, "Competency-Based Versus Traditional Cohort-Based Technical Education: A Comparison of Students' Perceptions," *Journal of Career and Technical Education*, Vol. 17, No. 1, Fall 2000, pp. 5–22.

Nagaoka, Jenny, Melissa Roderick, and Vanessa Coca, *Barriers to College Attainment: Lessons from Chicago*, Washington, D.C.: Center for American Progress, January 2009.

O'Donoghue, Tom, and Elaine Chapman, "Problems and Prospects in Competencies-Based Education: A Curriculum Studies Perspective," *Educational Research and Perspectives*, Vol. 37, No. 1, 2010, pp. 85–104.

Ochoa, Eduardo M., "Guidance to Institutions and Accrediting Agencies Regarding a Credit Hour as Defined in the Final Regulations Published on October 29, 2010," email letter to colleagues, Washington, D.C.: U.S. Department of Education, 2011. As of August 18, 2015: http://ifap.ed.gov/dpcletters/GEN1106.html

Ordonez, Bonnie, "Perspectives in AE—Competency-Based Education: Changing the Traditional College Degree, Power, Policy, and Practice," *New Horizons in Adult Education and Human Resource Development,* Vol. 26, No. 4, October 2014, pp. 47–53.

Person, Ann E., Lisbeth Goble, and Julie Bruch, *Developing Competency-Based Program Models in Three Community Colleges*, Oakland, Calif.: Mathematica Policy Research, April 30, 2014.

Pew Research Center, *Is College Worth It? College Presidents, Public Assess Value, Quality and Mission of Higher Education*, Washington, D.C.: Pew Social and Demographic Trends, May 16, 2011.

Porter, Stephen R., and Kevin Reilly, *Competency-Based Education as a Potential Strategy to Increase Learning and Lower Costs*, Washington, D.C.: HCM Strategists, July 2014.

Senate Bill (S.B.) No. 215, *Relating to the Continuation and Functions of the Texas Higher Education Coordinating Board, Including Related Changes to the Status and Functions of the Texas Guaranteed Student Loan Corporation*, Austin, Tex.: Texas State Legislature. As of August 12, 2015: http://www.legis.state.tx.us/tlodocs/83R/billtext/pdf/SB00215F.pdf#navpanes=0

Shapiro, Joel, "Competency-Based Degrees: Coming Soon to a Campus Near You," commentary, *Chronicle.com*, February 14, 2014. As of December 10, 2014: http://chronicle.com/article/Competency-Based-Degrees-/144769

Silva, Elena, Taylor White, and Thomas Toch, *The Carnegie Unit: A Century-Old Standard in a Changing Education Landscape*, Stanford, Calif.: Carnegie Foundation for the Advancement of Teaching, January 2015.

Southern Association of Colleges and Schools Commission on Colleges (SACSCOC), "Substantive Change for SACSCOS Accredited Institutions," policy statement, *SACSCOS.org*, June 2009. As of August 12, 2015: http://www.sacscoc.org/pdf/081705/SubstantiveChange.pdf

Sturgis, Chris, "Lesson Learned: Enabling Policy Isn't Enough, It Takes Incentives," *CompetencyWorks.org*, July 7, 2015. As of July 9, 2015: http://www.competencyworks.org/policy /lesson-learned-enabling-policy-isnt-enough-it-takes-incentives

U.S. Congress, 109th Cong., 1st Sess., Deficit Reduction Act of 2005 (Public Law 109-171), 2006, Washington, D.C.: H.R. 4241, February 8, 2006.

U.S. Department of Education, *Applying for Title IV Eligibility for Direct Assessment (Competency-Based) Programs (GEN-13-10)*, March 19, 2013. As of August 12, 2015: http://ifap.ed.gov/dpcletters/GEN1310.html

U.S. Department of Education, *Competency-Based Education Programs—Questions and Answers*, December 19, 2014. As of August 12, 2015: http://ifap.ed.gov/dpcletters/GEN1423.html

U.S. Department of Education, *Notice Inviting Postsecondary Educational Institutions To Participate in Experiments Under the Experimental Sites Initiative; Federal Student Financial Assistance Programs Under Title IV of the Higher Education Act of 1965, as Amended*, Federal Register 79 FR 44429, July 31, 2014, pp. 44429–44436. As of September 9, 2015: https://www.federalregister.gov/articles/2014/07/31/2014-18075/notice-inviting -postsecondary-educational-institutions-to-participate-in-experiments-under-the

U.S. Department of Education, National Center for Education Statistics (NCES), "Tables 326.10 and 326.20," *The Condition of Education 2015* (NCES 2015-144), annual report, May 28, 2015. As of August 18, 2015: https://nces.ed.gov/fastfacts/display.asp?id=40

White House, "College Scorecard," *Whitehouse.gov*. As of December 15, 2014: http://www.whitehouse.gov/issues/education/higher-education/college-score-card

White House, "Fact Sheet: The President's Plan to Make College More Affordable: A Better Bargain for the Middle Class," news release, Washington, D.C.: Office of the Press Secretary, August 22, 2013. As of December 10, 2014: http://www.whitehouse.gov/the-press-office/2013/08/22 /fact-sheet-president-s-plan-make-college-more-affordable-better-bargain-

White House, "Fact Sheet: White House Unveils America's College Promise Proposal: Tuition-Free Community College for Responsible Students," news release, Washington, D.C.: Office of the Press Secretary, January 9, 2015. As of March 20, 2015: https://www.whitehouse.gov/the-press-office/2015/01/09 /fact-sheet-white-house-unveils-america-s-college-promise-proposal-tuitio

Wooten, Kevin C., and Max Elden, "Cogenerating a Competency-Based HRM Degree: A Model and Some Lessons from Experience," *Journal of Management Education*, Vol. 25, No. 2, April 2003, pp. 231–257.